Singing Out Loud

Singing Out Loud

A Memoir of an
Ex–Mardi Gras Queen

Marilee Eaves

She Writes Press, a BookSparks imprint
A Division of SparkPointStudio, LLC.

Published 2019
Printed in the United States of America

ISBN: 978-1-63152-666-4
ISBN:. 978-1-63152-667-1
Library of Congress Control Number: 2019906553

For information, address:
She Writes Press
1569 Solano Ave #546
Berkeley, CA 94707

She Writes Press is a division of SparkPoint Studio, LLC.

All company and/or product names may be trade names, logos, trademarks, and/or registered trademarks and are the property of their respective owners.

Names and identifying characteristics have been changed to protect the privacy of certain individuals.

I dedicate this book to my husband,

Edwin James,

my sweet rock for the past twenty-eight years.

Contents

PREFACE

Ten years ago, I started writing down vignettes that developed into personal stories. I wanted to share the bumps and nudges, prods and prompts that led to my awakening from a decades-long struggle to carve out a place for my well self. And to evolve. In these pieces, I shared my vulnerability, and that helped me take steps to move forward. Those pieces developed into this book, in which I describe how, over time, I came to my senses. From my wartime infancy in Uptown Mardi Gras–saturated New Orleans to three months before Katrina, when I took refuge in the ancient fir forests of the Northwest, I tell stories of obsession, unholy judgment, and grief.

Raw and sometimes funny, my tumultuous journey tells of breaking the trance of the New Orleans tribe I adored, learning to trust my intuition, and building a new community of healing. Written out of my curiosity, bright outlook, struggles with alcoholism and bipolarity, joyful sense of adventure, and desire to find my groundedness, these stories are connected by grace.

Note well: While most of the names in this book are real, a few have been changed.

Chapter 1

The Summons

In early spring of 1962, while I was living in a locked ward at McLean Hospital, no longer hallucinating, in therapy every day and recovering from the psychotic break that had landed me there, an attendant came to my room to tell me I had a phone call. He walked me to the telephone closet down the hall, where I picked up the dangling receiver. "Marilee," my mother said, "you've been invited to be Queen of the Krewe of Osiris Ball for next year's debutante season!" She was so excited. I could hear it in the upbeat pitch of her voice.

"Mom, I'm in McLean. What are you thinking?"

"Marilee, we think it would be a great way for you to come home." I could hear the determination in her voice. But she sounded so far away.

My heart shrank as I realized she had no idea that what she was asking me to do was absurd, not to mention dangerous. She believed it was in my best interest to go home for the balls, pick up the thread of my life, and fold myself back into the tradition. She hadn't a clue what leaving a psych ward to attend a fake royal bash might do to me. She didn't know what she was asking of me. But she insisted, nonetheless.

"But you'll make your debut! Yes, there will be heavy commitments, and you'll have to fly down from Boston for all the events. It'll be wonderful. Just like it was for me. You'll start in August. That's when the deb parties begin, and all the debs are featured in *The Times-Picayune*. Then there are two large presentations of the debs on Thanksgiving weekend, more presentations during the Carnival season from Twelfth Night, or January sixth, until the stroke of midnight on Mardi Gras, March 6th this year."

I didn't know much about the Krewe of Osiris, but I understood that, like any Mardi Gras krewe, this krewe would put on balls with monarchs, a tableau, masked dancers, and gowned guests. As their queen, I would have to follow a punishing schedule of dress fittings and presentations and parties and balls that would demand a commitment of time and energy I didn't know if I could muster. This would require me to play a role they had chosen for me at a time when I was struggling to figure out who I was. It would be several months before I could leave the hospital, and I had no idea what shape I'd be in or how I would navigate post-hospital life, how I would manage to maintain a therapy schedule, a full slate of college classes, and buying groceries. Was I going to be able to do this?

"Mom, do you really think this is a good idea?"

"Marilee, the Krewe of Osiris made a formal request for you to be their queen this year, as an honor to your grandfather. Your grandfather, your father, your stepfather, your cousins, the whole family will be so disappointed if you don't accept," she said. "It's an honor for the family as much as for you."

My grandfather, E.O., was an influential member of the New Orleans community and well known in Mardi Gras circles. He had started in the cotton business in New Orleans at the age of sixteen, worked his way from messenger boy to principal cotton trader for the whole city, and made a mint, or so I've been told. And in the middle of the Great Depression, E.O. donned an ermine-trimmed train and white tights to reign as Rex, King of Carnival, with Nain, my grandmother, cheering him on. As I thought of him wearing his crown and waving his scepter to the crowds of people below him as they watched the Rex parade go by, his big smile shining above his pasted goatee, I remembered the day my cousins, my sister Pixie, and I discovered his crown and scepter in the attic, waking me up to the seduction and splendors of Mardi Gras and its celebrations. I'd nursed a fantasy of one day being crowned queen and wielding a scepter of my own. Pixie and I had returned home from our weekly visit with Daddy's family late one Sunday afternoon in 1950, when my cousins Lawrie and Malcie joined us and discovered the treasures in the attic of my grandparents' house on Loyola Avenue.

"Let's go up to the third floor," Lawrie, one year my senior, said, "and see what we can find! We can sneak up there without them hearing us." Lawrie drew up all of his four feet eleven inches and beckoned to us girl cousins to follow him to the upstairs back hallway. Brown-haired and wiry, he had the pale skin of a redhead. At nine, he was the oldest in our tight little group and liked to boss us girls around, but he was fun, and I didn't mind much. I was eight, Malcie almost eight, and Pixie seven. We followed him, huddled gleefully in a rough circle— ready for some adventure. We ran past the adults already holding toddies in their hands and followed him up the stairs.

Lawrie gingerly turned the knob of the door to the attic and placed his tennis-shoed foot on the first step of the steep wooden stairs. Pixie went next, then Malcie, and I brought up the rear. When I had previously asked what was behind this door, my grandmother had said, "You're not allowed in the attic.

Pocky is the only person who can go up there," ending the conversation. Pocky, aka Arthur Bradford, and his wife, Octavia, worked for my grandparents. I had known Pocky all my life as my grandparents' servant.

We knew Pocky was downstairs serving drinks to our parents, so we didn't have to worry about him stopping us. And creeping up together in a pack made it easy to disregard the rule. We crawled up the narrow stairs one after the other, past a mop and bucket, scrub brushes and rags for cleaning bedrooms and bathrooms on the second floor, wooden tennis rackets, cans of balls, badminton racquets, and birdies. What else would we find up here? I chewed my lip, a little nervous about going into the darkish, off-limits upper reaches of the house.

I briefly imagined that the grownups were downstairs in the living room, standing around the highly polished brass fireplace guardrail, drinks in hand, a lively fire giving off a woody smell that blended with the faint perfume of the signature scent of one of my female relatives, but I can't remember whose. In Nainnain and E.O.'s house, five o'clock signaled the cocktail hour, with or without company. My grandfather was probably sitting in his cognac leather chair under a portrait of Winston Churchill, drinking his toddy, fiddling with one of his pungent pipes, his legs crossed, revealing a slender ankle and garter, his bright blue eyes sparkling. He always faced away from the portrait of his deceased son that shined out over the room. I never saw him look at it.

I knew Pocky, dressed in his white, stiffly pressed butler's jacket, linen napkin carefully folded over his forearm, would be entering from the kitchen pantry to serve E.O. his bourbon from an octagonal silver tray with a smile that bespoke comfortable familiarity—the perfect butler playing his role—and then he would serve the others. I wonder, did Pocky take a deep breath before entering the living room? Was he extraordinarily skilled at playing the role of devoted butler in order to make a living? If so, he was a good actor.

Octavia, slight with thin ankles but large bosomed, would be standing in the kitchen, heaving her usual audible sigh as she arranged cutout circles of crustless watercress sandwiches and bacon-wrapped water chestnuts on another silver tray for Pocky to pass around. Octavia's presence provided a divine buffer between us and the adults who were too busy drinking and talking to think about what the children were up to. While Pocky and Octavia served them downstairs, we kids felt free to poke about. I doubt we would have ventured into the attic without this window of unsupervised time.

And there, leading our adventurous pack up the attic stairs, was Lawrie, who landed noisily on a thin piece of plywood at the top of the steps and stage-whispered to us girls, "Come on up. There's plenty of light from the front window."

I could see enough to step on the first two-by-four and then the next and the next until I stood at the front attic window, all glass from far above my head to my knees. It was weird to look down on narrow Loyola Avenue, lined with oaks and crepe myrtles, from so high up. I could peer into the upper windows of the house across the street and into the branches of the large oak tree in the lot next door.

I turned around and caught Pixie and Malcie gleefully hopping from one attic floor beam to the next. Blue-eyed Pixie was something of a very pretty tomboy—so pretty, people just liked to look at her. She loved a bit of mischief, showing up unafraid and full of spunk. She and I shared a room. She was neat with her things, smart, and read until we had to turn the lights out. She was different from me, with my sturdy legs, hazel-brown eyes, and thick brown hair. She did not express her emotions openly the way I did, and I thought she was the apple of E.O.'s eye.

"Shush, you all!" I turned toward some hanging garment bags, paused for a second, unzipped one, and discovered one of my grandmother's beaded ball dresses. Such pretty fabric! Pale blue, soft, and substantial. In the dim light, I could make out a scooped neck and the beads around it glistening with the light reflected from the front window. I fantasized about finding more dresses to touch and try on, sparkling in a long gown. But two more bags yielded only heavy wool suits. I felt gypped. And I wasn't up for jumping across the two-by-four beams.

"This floor is scary," I said to no one in particular.

About that time, Malcie, the adventurous one, called out to the rest of us from deep in a corner, bending over a large, pale, yellow-green box about fifteen inches high. I made my way over to her, thankful not to fall between the beams.

"Ouch, my head!" I'd hit the upper interior surface of the slanted roof. I held my hand over the bump, stooped down, and examined the outside of the faded chartreuse velvet box for myself. It was hinged, about the size of two of Nain's sofa cushions stacked one on top of the other.

Malcie opened the clamshell-shaped box and shrieked, "Look at this!" What did I smell? It was so dusty.

"Wow!" Pixie and I said simultaneously.

Lawrie moved in close to the box, eyes wide open as he stood up and knocked his head. "Ouch!"

A man-sized crown and a slender metal stick covered in gold tones and rhinestones—I would later learn it was called a scepter—sparkled at us invitingly from the ivory velvet lining of the case, which was musty from being stored away for more than a decade. I moved in gingerly, careful of my footing, drawn to this fairy-tale object that summoned thoughts of royalty and shone even in this dark attic. Images of kings and castles, queens and princesses leapt into my mind. This was a real crown!

With some self-importance, Lawrie explained that this must be E.O.'s crown and scepter from the day he was Rex, King of Carnival—before any of us were born. "He must have worn this when he led the Rex parade through the city! Mom told me all about this." He lifted the crown from its fittings and placed it on his head. "My mom was queen a few years after E.O. was king." Awkwardly, he waved the long, decorated stick back and forth in the limited attic space, a silly, joyful grin on his face. The shaft of the slender scepter looked like white gold and was topped with imitation diamonds that seemed real to me.

"I'd like to try it," said Pixie, hopping up and down.

Lawrie handed the crown and scepter to Pixie, ignoring his red-haired sister. When Pixie put the crown on her head, it slipped down over her face. She managed to swing the scepter from left to right, then yielded it to Malcie, who slipped on the headpiece and, pushing it up away from her face, broke out in a big grin as she waved the magic wand.

"My turn, y'all!" I cried. I was surprised—the crown felt as weighty as a stack of books. And it didn't fall down on my good-sized head. I gripped the scepter and touched Pixie lightly on the head, as if knighting her. I waved the wand back and forth clumsily and laughed out loud. I liked the feeling of power surging through my body.

Malcie clapped her hands and said, "You're a queen!" Pixie balanced on a beam and grinned. I wanted to know more about why my grandfather had this crown and scepter and what it meant to be King of Carnival. I had so many questions. Why had he been chosen for this? Had he had to pay for it? Had he gotten to pick his own queen? How did one become a queen? Where had the dresses come from? And where had Nainnain been in all this? Had she been the queen to his king?

Lawrie yelled, "Watch out for the overhead beam!" as I strutted around from one floor beam to another in a rush of elation, grinning at the others, throwing back my shoulders. Lawrie stood with his hand out, on tenterhooks, so I passed the crown and scepter back to him. He accepted it carefully and said, "I'll take another turn while I can."

"E.O. must be a special person," I said, *and so I must be special too.* My disappointment at not finding more ball gowns in the attic melted away, replaced by the joy and shushed hooting of clandestine play.

For that hour, stepping across the attic floor boards in my grandparents' attic, surrounded by Pixie and my cousins, I forgot worrying about whom my mother would marry and, my greatest fear, moving out of Nain's house where I felt so safe. Focusing on kings and queens bypassed the confusion and pain of being part of a broken family and not knowing who I was.

I liked the idea of carrying on a tradition that my family embraced. I felt a warmth settle in my stomach just thinking about my family's friends and acquaintances, belonging to a group. Little did I know that the life of make-believe kings and queens required a prescribed etiquette and would take on a different connotation for me in a little over a decade.

Standing in the attic, I sang the words of what had become the Carnival anthem shortly after the 1872 visit of a Russian aristocrat to the New Orleans Carnival: "If Ever I Cease to Love, If Ever I Cease to Love, May the Grand Duke Alexis ride a pony into Texas, If Ever I Cease to Love." I remembered the flag I had seen hanging from a long pole in front of my grandparents' house during Mardi Gras season—purple, gold, and green on a cream background with an embroidered crown in the center and the year of E.O.'s reign appliquéd in the corner.

Suddenly, I heard, "Whoa, what was that?" Pocky's voice rose above the din, and the dreams flew out the attic window. Our play came to a halt. "Mr. Lawrie, Miss Marilee, Miss Malcie, Miss Pixie, come down here right now. You'n supposed to be

up in the attic, no way. Get outta there. Your parents are callin'
you. Come downstairs right now!"

"Whoops, time to go," Lawrie said.

I yelled down the stairs, "Pocky, we're comin'! Please don't
tell 'em where we've been. We'll behave."

I took one last longing look at the velvet box. Pocky, attic
guardian, caught in between, stood in the hall near the door
until I, the last one of us down from the attic, firmly closed the
door—but not before I saw the curl of his mouth and glimpsed
a suppressed smile.

Remembering that magical day in the attic, I found myself
intrigued at the thought of wearing a crown and wielding a
scepter—now, as an adult. As I stood in the hallway at McLean,
my mother at the other end of the call, all those young dreams
of being a queen were reawakened in me. I recalled the photograph I had once found in Nain's desk drawer, showing her
dressed as Queen of the Mystick Ball. She was walking regally
down a white canvas path that had been laid out before her,
wearing an elegant gown with a long train, and accompanied
by six debutantes in gowns almost as beautiful as hers. And
another image—this one of my mother as Queen of the Mystery Ball, wearing a bejeweled crown and holding a scepter. I,
too, could be a queen. Dreaming of this, I pushed aside the
sense that the make-believe life of kings and queens required a
punishing schedule and strict etiquette, and that it demanded
I play a role laid out for me. I pushed aside my doubts about
whether I'd be able to do it without falling apart. To see the look
on E.O.'s face when I walked as a queen might be worth all the
trouble and risk. And, still in recovery in McLean, still finding
my way, my voice, myself, I couldn't say no when my mother, my
family, my tradition summoned me home. Saying no to them
was not an option.

Chapter 2

$\mathcal{D}$EX $\mathcal{D}$IARIES

I think my family had been preparing me to take my place in the family tradition and grooming me for the possibility of being a queen my whole life. From our life in New Orleans to the summers spent at E.O. and Nain's summer compound in Biloxi, I was constantly being molded for the role I was to play.

My grandparents' Biloxi compound was a magical place for my sisters, my cousins, and me. The 1847 red brick house sat far back from a long white picket fence. It was side-gabled, two stories, with upstairs and downstairs galleries stretching wide across the front. From the upper gallery and from the swimming pool through the fringed branches of the venerable three-hundred-year-old towering oak tree, you could see Deer Island a mile away in the Gulf of Mexico. In high summer we had our rituals—swimming in the pool, climbing trees, playing hide and seek all over the four acres, and tying scrap meat to round nets for crabbing off the pier across the coastal highway. We feigned afternoon naps while Nainnain took her rest, sat at the table together and ate Octavia's delicious fresh food, rocked in the big hammock mesmerized by the moving patterns of oak branches against blue skies, and on rainy days built forts with upside-down rockers. I felt secure under my grandmother's management.

Summers in Biloxi, I was Nain's best helper.

"You're my angel," Nainnain said as we crossed the grounds carrying dirty glasses from the swimming pool to the main house. As we walked past Pixie, Malcie, and Lawrie, who were taking turns hanging from a trapeze under the Osage orange tree, I felt a tug to be with them. But I changed my mind when we passed the towering oak tree on our way in from the pool, and Nainnain said, "Your ears should be burning. Dr. Esh says you're his favorite." I felt embarrassed at being singled out this way, but I liked Dr. Esh, short for Eshleman. He and his wife, long-time friends of my grandparents, were guests in the red-shingle house on the property. Seventy-five, but seeming much younger, Dr. Esh tickled my funny bone. He'd stand on his head in the grass and walk around the shallow end of the pool, cupping his fingers, creating waterspouts, and making squeaky noises while the other adults sat around an umbrella table, smoking and drinking Cokes or toddies. He enjoyed himself and broke with tradition—an odd duck. I liked him for that. Thinking of what Nain had said, I suppose Dr. Esh and I admired the quirkiness in each other.

Nainnain pulled her wide straw hat from her head. "I'm glad you're helping me get the supper ready," she said, opening the screen door. I nodded. "We've got a big crowd, and I can use your assistance."

I followed my grandmother into the kitchen and put the unwashed glasses in the sink, suppressing my desire to go play with the others. As the oldest female grandchild present, I was always encouraged by my mom to help with snacks and supper. It was expected, and I didn't mind lending a hand. Nainnain really did need me, and I needed her just as much. The words of praise in her calm voice always soothed me, and I felt a warm glow. I loved that she seemed unshakeable and delivered no surprises. My shoulders loosened as she asked me to take Cokes and a bowl of crackers out to the pool. I felt more at ease around her than the other adults, even my own mother.

A few days later, I was on my way to take a swim, anticipating a dive into the deep, shaded end of the pool. I saw Dr. Esh heading for the pool and wondered what funny thing he would reveal that day. Mrs. Eshleman was walking from the rear screen door of the red-shingle house toward the steps to the raised pool, her five-foot figure outlined against the bamboo growing along the property line to her left. She wore a lavender linen sheath dress and canvas sling-back shoes, her bluish-gray hair rolled tightly in a neat curve at the nape of her neck. She carried a tray of Coca-Colas, beads of condensation forming on the green bottles. Spotting me, she called for help, nearly dropping her tray. I hurried over. She chattered away, holding her tray out to me, pushing it closer. I grabbed it from her, staggering under its weight, which she ignored.

Walking alongside me, she wiped her pale white brow, talking at a fast clip. "The adults will be delighted to have something to drink. I'm so glad you can help me, I'm almost faint from the heat."

I cringed at her shrill voice. Biting my tongue to hold back what I really wanted to say, I smiled and said, "Yes, Mrs. Eshleman," and then headed for the pool with the tray, yelping each time my bare foot stepped on a rockachaw, the coastal sandbur that infiltrated the lawn, wishing I had worn sandals. The sharp stings from the brittle flowers shocked my whole body, not just my feet, and I almost lost it. My aunt Malcolm, Malcie's mother, noticed my plight and hopped out of her chair to meet me on the steps leading up to the pool terrace. She took the tray from my hands. "That's so heavy with all these Coke bottles," she said, smiling. "Thanks, Marilee, for helping out."

I sighed, relieved and grateful for the help and her thanks. As the stinging subsided, I walked to the other end of the pool under a low branch of the big oak tree and dove into the clear amber artesian water, the unusual color probably stemming from iron or clay. No one else was in the pool and, being pretty far from the adults sitting on the terrace at the other end, I pulled down my bathing suit top, feeling the joy of cool water rippling over my chest. For a few stolen minutes, I shut my eyes and imagined my legs bound in a single scaly sheath, gliding through the water, my tiny buds bobbing under the surface, the angle of the water making them appear larger than reality. I liked the delicious pressure of the water against my skin, the feeling of weightlessness. The bliss of it! But the thought of the people at the other end of the pool prompted me to force my eyes open, pull up my straps, and release the mermaiden sheath binding my legs.

My mother's voice pierced my reverie. "Marilee, run into the house and get my glasses, won't you?" She sounded sweet in front of everyone.

I sighed and climbed out of the deep end to accommodate her. After all, she had just taken me shopping for a bathing suit, even if she had made a big deal of picking out one that made me look thinner.

I grew up a world-class people pleaser, but try as I might, I felt I could never please my mother. When my sister Penny came along, with her high-spirited nature and disregard for such niceties, it was a little shocking to me and probably to Pixie. I could laugh outright at Dr. Esh's antics, but my baby sister's boldness unnerved me—that impudence that I envied and couldn't imagine emulating.

When I was almost ten years old, Mom married Albert Bruce Crutcher Jr., whom we called Crutcher. He had transplanted to

New Orleans from Texas, where he'd worked in the oil business. In New Orleans, he continued to work in the same industry, eventually starting his own company with a partner. When he walked into our lives in pursuit of my mother, my whole world changed, for better and for worse. The beginning was definitely rough. A month or so before they were married, Crutcher invited all of us kids and Mom to go to a movie. We were supposed to depart from Nainnain's house at three o'clock, but at 2:50, I had a sudden attack of constipation. Barely able to move, I crawled to the small bathroom I shared with my mother and sisters.

I lay on the white tile floor, writhing in pain, surrounded by lemon-yellow walls, a slight breeze ruffling the short pressed white cotton curtains on the open window. Nainnain's maid knelt down, talking to me softly to help me relax, and Nain stood by. Mom came to the bathroom and stood in the doorway, briefly, but she gritted her teeth the whole time, knowing that Crutcher and the others were waiting downstairs, ready to go. I felt so embarrassed, humiliated, and wildly frustrated that I was late for the outing. But I was stuck, mortified, unable to straighten up.

Within three minutes, Mom announced she would go on with the others without me. I stayed home and missed the first special outing with Crutcher. Misery was my name, misery and shame. That body of mine. I don't know if Mom told Crutcher why I'd delayed the party, but I felt awkward around him for quite a while after (just the beginning of the discomfort I would feel around Crutcher until the day I said goodbye), sucking in my stomach whenever we were in the same room.

In the spring of 1952, Crutcher and my mother married in a civil ceremony in my grandparents' living room, witnessed by four of their friends, the portrait of my mother's deceased little brother looking down on them. E.O. and Nainnain were away on their yacht. Octavia came upstairs and helped us brush our messy hair and put on our best pajamas over full-blown chickenpox. Then Pocky and Octavia looked on from the dining room doorway in their uniforms, hands folded, smiling, while we girls sat on the carpeted steps and gaped at our gorgeous mother. We weren't about to miss her wedding by staying upstairs in bed, and she was too busy downstairs to keep us away. I thought she was beautiful in a pale blue linen suit and a tiny hat with a fern-green veil. Crutcher, with his big presence, cut a handsome figure in a white linen suit, his half-gold front tooth gleaming in the afternoon sunlight that filtered through the windows.

After they returned from their Caribbean honeymoon, we three daughters with Mom moved into Crutcher's two-room apartment. My excruciating self-consciousness and embarrassment from wearing pajamas in front of this stranger mitigated itself with the hilarity of jumping on three beds pushed together in the one bedroom of Crutcher's place. After a couple of months adjusting to close quarters, the move to a larger apartment on Walnut Street overlooking the trees in Audubon Park felt freeing. By this time Mom was pregnant. Pixie and I had moved into a small bedroom painted bubblegum-pink off the kitchen pantry. We had matching white iron beds, slant top desks, and tall windows that looked out on the metal roof of parking garages.

It was clear before long that Crutcher ruled the roost by cajoling and persuading with his loud voice. "Marilee, you and Pixie can play tennis for five hours today. And figure out a plan for earning money this summer." And, in an almost inaudible voice, I would mumble my words on purpose because I didn't have a good enough answer.

A few months after moving into the Walnut Street apartment, Mom took me to the family pediatrician, Dr. Emile Naef, to talk about my "weight problem." I was ten at the time. I envied

Pixie her slight build, and Penny, my younger sister, age five, was a slender kid as well. I sat in the doctor's office silently shrinking into the sofa cushions, staring down at a leaf in the faded chintz pattern and feeling that familiar shame. Dr. Naef was Swiss but had moved to New Orleans when his daughter's family settled there. He touched his straw-colored, thinning hair, slicking it back with his fingers. *Does he pencil in those ginger eyebrows?* I wondered as he gestured to us to sit in chairs across his desk from him and asked how we were doing.

Almost immediately he said, "I know of a new way to help young ladies lose weight. I think you'll be astounded at its effectiveness." I never questioned him or my mother about why she thought I needed this treatment. I simply soaked up her and my stepfather's opinion that I needed to lose weight and figured this just fit into all the preparation for being a deb, a queen, a proper New Orleans society lady. So I took the Dexedrine and thyroid pills Dr. Naef prescribed for his "new way."

That fall, when I started sixth grade, I felt sped up with new energy from the Dexedrine, and I couldn't sleep well. At odd times my body felt like a buzzing bumblebee, unfamiliar and uncomfortable. On the bright side, my schoolwork was excellent. It was easy to pore over the books and focus for hours, and I loved the attention I received for doing well. In fact, it became the only praise I could count on. And did I become thinner? Yes, just as most preadolescent girls do when stretching into their almost-eleven-year-old skins.

Over the years, I made regular trips to Dr. Naef's woodpaneled office and treatment room, housed in his family's hundred-year-old cottage. During each visit, the same routine unfolded. I'd sit on a rattan chair or the faded chintz sofa in the long reception hallway with its high ceilings, staring out at the crepe myrtles growing near the windows, waiting for Dr. Naef's receptionist to call my name, and when she did, I experienced the inevitable tightening in my gut as I slowly stood up to follow her. Chatting away, she'd lead me through the double, half-glazed doors to the doctor's office, while Mom remained in the hallway leafing through magazines or reading a book, sometimes with a baby in tow—or pregnant with another. Mom seemed always either newly pregnant, about to give birth, or carrying a newborn.

Everything in Dr. Naef's office appeared to be a variation on the color brown—the bead-planked walls, the old wide pineboard floor, the two dark-brown oriental rugs, the few hard wooden chairs—and he himself wore putrid brown silk suits. On each visit, I knew I'd see that ultra-cheerful but impersonal smile plastered on his face, along with the gleam in his eye, looking as though he were trying to get me to buy something. He'd direct me to enter his treatment room off to the right—white paint over beaded board—while delivering identical questions and comments every time.

"How are you, my dear Marilee? Yes, yes, you look marvelous. Sit here on this table." He'd poke in my mouth, nose, and ears with a flat wooden stick while I sat politely (of course) but warily, wondering how many pounds I would register that day. When he finished, I'd hop down from the table and stand on his tall scale. As he moved the metal slider, I felt I might die of suspense before it settled into place. He fussed at me if I'd gained, praised me if I'd dropped a few pounds. Either way, I stayed quiet while my stomach churned and my throat and cheeks burned. It's curious to me today why, on the one hand, I was so obedient, and on the other, so untrusting. What was clear was that I didn't know how to escape that conflict within me.

Year after year, I took the prescription refill, and Mom and I dropped it at the prescription counter of Katz & Besthoff, whose ubiquitous purple oval sign dotted the map of New Orleans. Some of what went on around this "weight problem" I mistrusted—at times I truly thought I looked just fine—but as I had so little trust in myself, I kept quiet.

Dr. Naef wasn't the only person who asked me to step on scales. Soon after he married my mother, Crutcher started weighing me every morning. When I think about those mornings, the small white hexagonal floor tiles below the scales flash in front of my eyes. I would stare at the black lines around each tile and start counting the tiles to keep my mind focused away from the shame of standing on the scales for Crutcher. I was doing what he asked, even though it seemed odd and wrong.

Crutcher was good-looking, enthusiastic, loud, and firm in his convictions of how things should be done. He was well intentioned, but his Marine pilot training and zero experience with parenting caused a degree of pain that he didn't intend unless he thought it was character building. Perhaps because he was an only child, he demanded the attention of all of us. I don't know. I do know I often felt confused and ashamed around this new father figure, as if the wind were being sucked out of me, joy eclipsed. A large-boned man, his big, raw physical energy and loud voice dominated the apartment, so different from that of either my father or grandfather, who were known more for their courtliness and elegance. They were Southern men, not cowboy Texans. I was still going with Daddy to his mother Sissy's on Sundays, but I felt he never embraced his role as a father. As I didn't see Daddy any other time, for the most part, Crutcher willingly filled that void in his own inexperienced way.

Standing on the scale, my anxiety level would rise as predictably as the sun. Every morning, Crutcher conducted my weigh-in as if he were doing me the greatest favor. My daily dose of shame despite his blustery encouragement. Before school each morning, still in my pajamas, he would shoo me into his and Mom's bathroom. "Hop on the scale," he'd say, sticking *The Times-Picayune* under his arm, taking a sip of the black coffee and chicory Mom brought him, and whipping out a small note-book and golf-scoring pencil from the bathroom cabinet. "How much today? One hundred thirty-two. Good work. Down one."

I'd watch the needle move and read the numbers that regis-tered. More often than not, when the needle went up or stayed the same, I'd burst into tears of frustration and shame—not knowing how to care for my sensitive self.

"Stop being so emotional!" Crutcher would say. "Stop cry-ing, for Christ's sake. This is for your own good."

I'd focus my eyes on Mom's rubber douche bag hanging over the towel rack above the tub. Not that I knew what it was. Some days, when Crutcher was out of town getting an oil land lease signed, Mom was in charge of my weigh-in. "Come on now," she'd say, her words clipped, "just stand on the scale and get it over with." Deep sigh. "Come on now, Marilee, I need to go get Allison and Penny ready for school." On those days, I felt abandoned by Mom, even though she was right in front of me. Other days I went numb, meaning, I think I just left my body.

I dreaded the routine, but there was no brooking this new practice. I never questioned, at least out loud, the weighing-in ritual and its effect on me or my siblings, or on my mother, for that matter. My mother's inexplicable collusion with Crutcher and Dr. Naef—really with the entire situation—galled me in later years, but during the years of weigh-ins, her participation in the ritual and her abandonment of me were just part of the morning nightmare.

Dinner around the square wooden table in the apartment presented some of the most mortifying times. Crutcher would pull himself up and wave his fork. "Marilee, you don't need to eat so much rice with your red beans. It'll show up on your thighs." Another time: "Whoops, no dessert for you. Pass it to one of your sisters." Mother would glare surreptitiously at me, as if to say, *Don't dare talk back to him.* One school friend who spent the night told me, embarrassed, that she couldn't come for supper anymore, because she couldn't stand how I was treated at the table.

I can't remember when the scales took a back seat. There were years of bizarre incidents, such as leaving the school lunchroom in the seventh grade to meet Mom in her car with lean, bunless hamburgers still warm in tin foil. We ate in the front seat of her maroon Chevrolet while my schoolmates sat in the wood-paneled dining room, enjoying black-eyed peas and rice and salad. When I weighed in over 135, in eighth grade, I was banned from going out with friends and kept from seeing a ninth-grade boyfriend. I can't remember if I was weighed in during vacations when I started boarding school at fifteen, but I continued taking the Dex and thyroid pills.

One day in eighth grade, Crutcher said, "I have a brilliant idea. Marilee, why don't you go to Bill Long's Bakery and eat as much as you want. Then you can go play handball for a few hours."

I acquiesced, shoulders folding in. I didn't know how to say no to him. In a corner of my mind, I heard a voice saying, *He does this for your own good.* And my chief skill, lest we forget, was still people pleasing.

We arrived at the bakery on Freret Street. I had often accompanied my mother there when shopping for a party or buying a king cake at Carnival time, and I had sometimes dreamed about the pastries behind those slanted glass counters.

We walked through the glass and metal door, a Coke machine on the left and L-shaped glass counters dominating the room, redolent with the smell of yeast and sugar. When Crutcher smiled and said, "Marilee, buy as many pastries as you want. Doughnuts, chocolate éclairs, brownies, Belgian slices. Here's some cash. Take your time," I only felt embarrassed. What was fun about being told to eat those goodies under these bizarre conditions?

Crutcher had rounded up my sister's boyfriend, also my friend and contemporary, blond and adorable, and hired him to be my workout coach for the day. Why in the world had he chosen this boy? I never asked, and I've never figured it out. Crutcher had instructed me to dress in sweat clothes despite the eighty-five-degree temperature. And to top it off, he'd invited a couple of family members to come along. The others were standing around the shop, my three-year-old brother Bruce running his finger along the length of one of the glass cases.

"And when you're done," Crutcher went on as he picked up the heavy box of goodies off the case and handed it to me, "I'll drive you two to the handball court at Tulane where you can hit balls for a few hours. In your sweat clothes."

What? I found myself watching the scene from afar, as though completely disconnected from my own body, from all feeling, unable to move—then felt humiliated. Here I was eating, or rather, bingeing in front of this cute boy and my family. Yet I felt torn. Part of me drooled at the thought of devouring these sweets, and I wanted to believe that this crazy plan could work to help me not eat so much—after all, Crutcher said it would—and part of me burned with shame and hurt to be targeted with this kind of attention. I bit into a chocolate éclair, then a couple of Belgian slices, a brownie, chocolate chip cookies, almond sugar cookie—and then I gagged. There were at least seven more in the white bakery box. No pleasure there.

At that time, I was a healthy 135 pounds. Not an ideal weight for a deb or a queen.

"Come on, Marilee," Crutcher urged as we walked by the case on the way out, "have another one. You don't have to skimp on this." I looked at the pastries behind the glass—delectable—but that was it for me. Stuffed, I climbed into his black Cadillac, that long, sleek car—it looked like a pimpmobile—he used to go looking for oil land leases. He delivered us with our rackets to the Tulane gymnasium and drove off with the younger kids.

Now my cheeks flushed. I was alone with this cute boy, Pixie's boyfriend, suddenly my coach. I had nothing to say. Fortunately, he was a kind and nonjudgmental soul and acted neither arrogantly nor unpleasantly. And so, dressed in sweats, we hit handballs against the wall for the next couple of hours. I quickly became dripping wet, exhausted, smelly, the shame detoxing out of my pores. As we left the courts, I wondered again if Crutcher's method would fix me. This was the only time I trained with someone, but during the next couple of years, the weighing continued, and I started playing five hours of tennis a day with my sister, at least in the summertime, always at Crutcher's encouragement. Years later, when I heard the term "binge and purge," I knew exactly what that meant.

When I was fifteen, Crutcher insisted that I go away to boarding school outside Baltimore. Mom was right there, sitting up ramrod straight at the square dining table when he made the pronouncement, dabbing her lips with her napkin, saying nothing. I silently implored her with my eyes but to no avail. *Well, that didn't work.* I felt pushed out, abandoned. By that time, we were a family of eight—two adults and six children (my baby brother John was only a year old) in the six-room Walnut Street apartment.

I knew a handful of girls going off to boarding school, but it was not the usual route to education experienced by a circle of girls who would in just a few years make their debuts in New Orleans society. But Crutcher had high academic standards for education and was determined that going away for school for me and my siblings would satisfy those standards and give us a valuable base for the rest of our lives. The diversity I experienced at school was geographical and economic rather than ethnic. At the time, I couldn't help but wonder about Crutcher's decision.

Even though the idea of escaping from the baby factory at home appealed to me, being sent to boarding school felt like a shove out of the family, into foreign territory, a place where I rarely felt happy, and away from my beloved New Orleans. But off I went to boarding school, completely outfitted with new uniforms and expensive riding jackets and jodhpurs—even though I knew nothing about riding—while the really good riders wore, guess what? Jeans!

During these high school years, I yearned to be part of the world that the attic treasure had introduced me to—Carnival balls and long gowns. And part of me assumed I *would* be, because of my family's affiliations. But I was confused. The price was high—all the humiliation of getting on the scale and taking drugs to lose weight. And something nagged at me about stepping into this hierarchical world, hunches I couldn't yet identify about glaring racial, economic, and social imbalances. But I'd spent years watching my mother get her hair done, make up her face, and dress up for the balls, and I couldn't help but look forward to my turn to take part. Clarity of thinking in this area was beyond my reach, and I didn't act on my perception of the disparities.

My confusion led to conflict. Part of me longed to belong and be the perfect deb, the queen in training, but another part of me rebelled against being forced into that role. I took the Dexedrine and thyroid pills from age ten through middle school and boarding school, my freshman year in college, and the summer after, and I kept on doing well in school. Along with my pill-induced anxiety—or had I always been somewhat anxious?—I continued to turn to sweet food for comfort. Our cook and babysitter, Ruth Nobles, who was close to my mother's age, slipped me peanut butter and grape jelly sandwiches on white bread, and didn't tattle on me when I snuck Cameos and Oreos out of the pantry closet, located next to the pink bedroom I shared with my sister. No wonder I wasn't losing weight! Ruth's constant and warm presence filled a need in our household. She gave warm hugs and functioned as a loving safe haven for me during those confusing times. I felt the underlying zinging in my body quiet down when she put her arms around me.

The summer after my sixteenth birthday, my rebellion took a different turn. I started sneaking out of the family apartment on Walnut Street early in the morning to meet with the twenty-six-year-old lifeguard from the New Orleans Lawn Tennis Club, a Tulane graduate English teaching assistant. At first I met him early mornings at the Tennis Club, and then I somehow got myself to his French Quarter apartment on St. Peter Street. I suppressed my guilt over the agitation I observed in Pixie, who knew of my sneaking out to meet this creep who was ten years older than I. He called me his "French Quarter chick" for more than a year—my junior year—and that simply meant his young girlfriend in the Quarter. I felt appreciated and exotic eating breakfast with him at The Coffee Pot, dining on steak and fries at a nearby steakhouse, and listening to modern jazz around the corner from his fourth-floor apartment in a dim and smoky joint. After I returned home for Christmas holidays from boarding school, he introduced me to *Tannhauser* and classical music, and I was enthralled. I seemed to garner more affection from him than I did at home—certainly more positive attention toward my young and curvy body, or so I thought—not an ideal situation, but with three babies at home, Mom barely had time to brush her teeth. I realized forty years later that, except for the statute of limitations, El Creep-O would have been subject to statutory rape charges because I was a minor. I had definitely crossed over the line from my Uptown breeding, but I'd had the opportunity to observe that plenty of people lived differently from family and friends at the New Orleans Lawn Tennis Club or the Country Club.

My mother tried to curb my rebellion the best she knew how. When I was seventeen, she made an appointment for me with an old schoolmate of hers, a neuropsychiatrist, Dr. Walter Trautman. She was vague about the purpose of the visit, saying only that it might help me lose weight. *A neuropsychiatrist?* She went into the doctor's office with me, and after some initial discussion, Dr. Trautman asked her to leave the room. He and I sat in silence for a couple of minutes before he said, "You know, this is not about you. This is about your family."

It's about your family. I stared at him, as if not hearing him, and then slowly, as his words sank in, I felt as if a cushion had been slipped under my head for the moment—I could rest peacefully, my neck muscles relaxed and fluid. It was the first time I considered that I might not be the problem, that although I was the person my family identified as the one who needed help, I was fine the way I was. I had felt such conflict about myself vis-à-vis my family, and here he was letting me know that I didn't have to be caught between the two, between what my family wanted me to be and my struggle to be myself. And I realized eventually that I didn't truly understand the importance of this until years later, so I continued feeling caught.

Chapter 3

COLD TURKEY

Thanks to the prompting of the neuropsychiatrist who understood me, Dr. Trautman, by the summer after my freshman year at Wellesley College—after nine years of dutifully taking daily prescribed doses of Dexedrine and thyroid pills—I felt I needed to do something differently. During that first year at Wellesley, I had continued taking my pills as prescribed. Wide-eyed and judgmental, I watched dorm mates indiscriminately toss back NoDoz, Stay Awake, Ex-Lax, or whatever it was they took to study all night for exams—ingesting anything that would help them focus or stay awake—and it bothered me. However, at that point, I didn't have the perspective to take a look at my own use of a stimulant. No wonder I didn't need NoDoz.

I spent most of that hot, sweaty summer of 1961 after my freshman year, the summer I turned nineteen, at my grandparents' Biloxi compound on the Mississippi Gulf Coast. Pocky and Octavia Bradford still worked for them. In Biloxi, they drove to my grandparents' house from their home in Back Bay, ready to work. However, when they worked in the city, they lived in a sparsely furnished apartment above Nain's double garage. Every morning, Pocky and Octavia would smile warmly when I entered my grandmother's kitchen—or, I should say, Octavia's kitchen—light gray oilcloth on the long worktable, gray utilitarian walls a slight shade darker. Pocky's eyes twinkled, always appearing kind and gentle. His dark hair was flecked with white, but his brown skin was unwrinkled. Octavia's wiry hair was smoothed back in a small bun, her warm spirit palpable as she quietly went about her cooking duties. I rarely saw Octavia away from the stove stirring a pot or the sink washing dishes. Here was a woman who had borne nine children, living away from them when she was in the city with my grandparents, appearing as cheerful as she could be.

Pocky and Octavia had imparted a steady presence in my grandparents' house for as far back as I can remember. Though they were privy to our daily lives, I had no idea about their lives away from ours. Not all of their nine children were still alive. I didn't know how some had died or what the living ones did for a living except for their son Arthur, who worked as caretaker at my grandparents' Biloxi property, and their oldest daughter Elmire, large-chested with slim ankles, who taught in the Biloxi public school system and came to the house to work after school. And Elmire's daughter, who accompanied Elmire to the house from time to time and babysat me when I was a toddler. A photo documents that young relationship—Octavia's granddaughter, twelve, carrying fifteen-month-old me around on her hip. She later moved to the Chicago area along with so many other African Americans from the South, moving hopefully toward freedom and a life free from bias, especially after the mechanical cotton harvesters started replacing manual cotton picking.

I lived with Nain in the spring of 1966 shortly after E.O. died. We generally ate our meals in her upstairs sitting room or in the kitchen from plates of food prepared by Octavia and left warming for supper. One evening, Octavia became ill, and Nainnain asked me to carry soup up to her above the garage. "Of course!" I said, glad to be of help. Balancing the covered soup dish, I walked down the kitchen steps into the driveway, around the camellia bushes to the door to their apartment over the stucco garage. I was sure the soup was chicken noodle or chicken rice straight out of a Campbell's soup can. *It won't taste as good as if Octavia cooked it*, I thought.

As I stood at their door, I remembered how I had rubbed up against the rough stucco when playing hide and seek with my cousins behind the tall privet bushes. Underneath the apartment, Nain's navy Cadillac was parked inside the double garage in front of my grandfather's no-longer-driven navy Jaguar. On the other side of the garage, edging the property line, built up high to catch the sun, stood an orchid greenhouse.

I knocked on the Bradfords' door, with its full panel of that frosted glass designed for privacy. After a minute or two, Pocky opened it, wearing a worn, plaid flannel shirt, bedroom slippers, and work pants. His hair was short and nappy light gray, the lines in his face soft. "Why, Miss Marilee," he said, nodding to the bowl of soup, "what do you have here? Come on up and bring this to Octavia."

I greeted Pocky and followed him up the dimly lit steps that turned sharply inside the corner of the building. A small, dust-caked window afforded little light—it faced out to the backs of fine houses on the block.

Octavia came into focus. Her *café au lait* skin lay smooth over her distinct cheekbones, more pronounced than ever, and her white hair, usually tied neatly in a bun at the nape of her neck, was spread out loose on her pillow, emphasizing her sparrow-like features. She appeared tiny in bed, eyes closed, her skin glistening with sweat.

I don't know what I had expected; I hadn't thought about it. I felt flush with embarrassment and discomfort and intrusive as a bull, cheeks on fire, hands sweating. The contrast between the comfort of my grandparents' home and the sparsely furnished room in which I now stood pulled at my heartstrings. Theirs was a long boxcar of a space, walls of uncovered two-by-fours, with a pair of small windows at one end facing the driveway and the house. A single chair stood next to a shabbily painted dresser. The walls were bare. I felt confused.

Pocky said softly, "This is nice of you to bring your Nain-nain's soup. Octavia will surely appreciate it."

I didn't know what to say. I gripped the bowl so tightly that the yellow liquid dribbled over the rim and onto my hand. I shifted from one foot to the other. I was trying to reconcile the Pocky and Octavia I knew in the big house with the unfinished bareness of this room. I gave the bowl to Pocky, who placed it carefully on the dresser. I called a soft goodbye to Octavia and waved to Pocky, saying I would let myself out. Of course, he followed me and saw me out the door, thanking me again.

"See you in the morning," I said. "I hope Octavia feels better soon." I stood still a couple of steps past the doorway at the bottom of the steps and took a deep breath. Then I retraced my steps past the privet bushes and headed toward the house, stumbling on the flagstone pavers in the darkness until I stepped into a pool of light shining off a lamp next to the kitchen door. My confusion stayed with me as I mounted the steps and entered the kitchen. The Bradfords were benevolent presences in my life, and to see Octavia this sick scared me. I couldn't imagine life without her. But more than that, my visit had set off questions I couldn't yet grasp. This was a dimension different from the one I had occupied in New Orleans and begun to explore in

Boston—blithely running off to the library researching the Arts and Crafts Movement, trekking off on a Newcomb Art School tour of Chicago museums and private collections (even collections so extensive that a Toulouse-Lautrec hung in the laundry room), and shopping at Neiman's for dresses. Was Octavia a churchgoer? Proud of her children? Where had she learned to cook so well? Where had she grown up? Who had watched her children when she was at Nainnain's? This world had always been there, but I'd seen only my own. It had never occurred to me to ask about theirs.

For now, it was still 1961, the summer after my freshman year of college, five years before I was to bring Octavia her soup above the garage. Nain and I, along with my mother and her brood, decamped from New Orleans, with Pocky and Octavia in tow, to the family's Biloxi compound. My role at the compound that summer was being my mother's nanny, helping her look after my little brothers, while my longtime summer friend Richie Keenan looked after my uncle's three boys. Pixie was in England, Penny was spending the summer at a North Carolina camp, and little sister Allison, ten years younger, was away at camp in Texas.

Days in Biloxi followed an established routine. We would wake up, eat breakfast with the kids, play outside, swim in the big pool, and sit down to lunch prepared by Octavia and served by Pocky. After lunch it was rest time, required by Nainnain as a must during the polio years, providing quiet, rest, and a break from the hot sun and activity. Later in my life, I would grow to see the value of this siesta, finally understanding why it had been a staple in my grandmother's day. Sometimes during that hour or so, I would take a book to a favorite faded green canvas lounge chair under the big live oak. That tree was at least three hundred years old, gnarled with branches bent with sharp turns upward and then down again. Spanish moss hung in bearded clumps. On the ground, moss grew on branches in the shadow of clustered, embracing leaves, and bark clung to the trunk in overlapping and oversized patches. Three feet up from the bottom of the tree, a cut mark exposed its honey-colored meat.

After rest period ended at three, the kids ran out onto the lawn to play ball in their bathing suits, ready to dive in at four o'clock pool time. Most days, Richie called out, "Who wants to be pitcher? Catcher?" Or, "A Coca-Cola to the one who grabs the nets and the bait. Let's go crabbing!" And sometimes, we started a game of hide-and-seek around the stout oak and behind the aspidistra leaves picked and stripped for whips, shouting and posturing raucously. I dipped into the deliciously cool artesian well pool water, watching the kids play from one corner of the shallow end, flicking away an occasional inch-long, black, stinging beetle. The boys plunged green painted metal chairs into the shallow end of the pool, same as I had done when younger, and happily swam through and around them underwater. I winced at the screechy sound of metal scraping against the concrete pool floor, and was soothed by the smell of jasmine growing on a nearby old covered well. The boys exploded out of the water, seeking air and bursting with laughter, and then climbed out, lined up poolside, and took turns folding themselves into human bombs, big grins on their faces, making the loudest and biggest splash possible.

Every afternoon at five o'clock, after Pocky and Octavia left for the day, Richie, my mother, and I fixed tall gin and tonics in the kitchen and brought our drinks to the living room, where the Gulf breezes sifted through the front and rear screen doors. The gin tasted bitter, but I felt grown up, and it didn't take long before I looked forward to those lime-accented drinks. Both Richie and I were oldest children, born six days apart, both earnest and responsible. He was the grandson of one of my grandparents' close friends who lived down the beach. We'd spent many summer hours in my grandparents' pool and on their grounds. He served in the Tulane ROTC, wore a flat top, and usually dangled a cigarette from his sunburned lips. When we talked, he looked at me when I spoke and didn't shift his gaze. He responded in a way that made me think he got me, and that was a gift, since I didn't have much of a voice at home and often felt on the outside, awkward and needy. I welcomed Richie as a brother. Being away from parties and bars in the city, I felt freer than I had in years, closer to myself, getting a taste of thinking for myself.

One evening, as the two of us stood on the front porch of the big house, he with an unlit cigarette between his thumb and index finger, I found myself telling him about my prescription pills and the family's focus on my weight, and how I often felt as if I didn't belong to my own people.

"That's crazy, Marilee," he said. "You don't have to put up with that. You've been brainwashed, intentionally or not, to think you're not okay. You're fine! You're more than fine."

My body relaxed. I felt the muscles in my shoulders soften, and I felt a little brighter, light pouring in. It felt good, even if I was just basking in his sunlight and not accessing my own. I took a cue from one of my boarding school teachers, who counseled continual questioning, and asked myself, *If these pills are supposed to make me lose weight, how come I haven't done so in nine years' time? If I really want to lose weight, then I need to stop putting so much food in my mouth. No one can do it for me, and no one can have so much power over me. It's time to get off these pills. Why not just throw them away?*

And I did. I stopped taking the Dexedrine and thyroid pills, cold turkey. All those pills prescribed by the good Swiss doctor in the brown silk suit. Not that I knew then what cold turkey was. Not that I knew the ramifications of going off certain drugs willy-nilly. Encouraged by Richie, I felt more sheepish—no, nuts!

angry!—about my unchallenged docility, feeling the shame rise within me, chagrined that I'd been so compliant for so long, attempting to do what was expected of me—by my mom, by the doctor, by my stepfather, and by myself—all because I'd believed them when they said that life would be better if I kept my weight down. Thank you, summer brother, for the mirror.

I quit taking the pills and don't remember missing them. I said goodbye to Richie and the peaceful Biloxi summer. Mom and I packed up the children and headed back to New Orleans, where she and I shopped for my sophomore year. As we moved from Town & Country, where she said queens' dresses were created, to Dress Circle, where I bought two new skirts, a sweater, and several blouses, outwardly I appeared calm, but my mind started racing. And soon it was zinging along with excitement as I went about folding and packing pieces of clothing in my suitcase, checking them off my list—cotton blouses and pullovers, the lavender one with a cowl neck, skirts and cardigan sweaters, my wide leather belt, a heavy coat, front-pleated slacks—and prepared to return to Wellesley. I told no one that I had stopped taking the pills; it hadn't occurred to me to do so. And before I stepped onto the plane, I became quieter than my usual self and barely talked to anyone, a shift away from the excited feelings I'd had only days before.

Chapter 4

THE BREAK

The day after saying my last goodbyes in New Orleans, rather emotionless now that I recall, I sat on the plane bound for Boston and felt an unfamiliar but purposeful intention. *I'm going somewhere very special and I have to get ready*, I heard myself thinking. When my plane landed in Boston, I took a shuttle to the campus. Two friends, Mary Esther and Nancy, had joined me in picking a fabulous two-room suite in our dorm for our sophomore year, overlooking treetops and sparkling Lake Waban. I arrived on campus and immediately settled into our suite. I situated my things on one of the three beds in the sleeping quarters and put my clothes away in one third of the closet space. I knew living there with my new suite-mates would be perfect. When Mary Esther and Nancy finally turned up, we sat on our beds talking excitedly about the coming year.

"Can you believe we succeeded in getting this suite with these windows overlooking this incredible view?" Mary Esther said, bouncing on the bed, her short, evenly cut hair moving with her. She was majoring in geology and had lived on my floor last year.

"Yeah," Nancy said, dancing over to the window, her blonde hair in a neat bun on her dancer's neck. "I can lean out the window and watch you two rowing on the lake without lifting a finger."

"And we have our own living room," I said. "I can read late without disturbing you."

"I'd say we're set up for a spectacular year," Mary Esther added.

There was a great deal to look forward to at school, and things were "up." Looking back, I recall feeling untouchable, special, unusually special, though oddly devoid of emotion. I didn't share with my suitemates my growing sense of distinctiveness.

But that feeling of "upness" gave way, unpredictably, to an equally intense "down." One minute I felt energetic and high, and the next I dove into inactivity and sat for hours in the rocking chair in our living room while Nancy and Mary Esther went about their student lives.

Early on during the first days back at Wellesley, I went out with an MIT student named Jon. On our first date, thanks to my increasingly jumping then unwinding mind, I silently and instantly decided he was a suitable partner for me and that I'd accompany him on his upcoming important trip to West Africa. I latched on to my picture of who he was and how he would fit into my life. My mind jumped from having dinner with him in Boston all the way to meeting him in West Africa and working side by side in the Peace Corps to create lasting change at the grassroots level. After the Peace Corps, we would be married, he would become president of the United States, and I would be First Lady. But first, I remember thinking, before I jaunted off to be with Jon, I wanted to be elected president of our sophomore class.

One day, while relaxing with my roommates in our living area, I told them, "I'm running for class president. I've always wanted to. And I'm going to take just the classes I want and not the courses Crutcher wants me to take." I didn't tell them I felt in my bones that I would be leaving for an extensive trip to West Africa before long. In retrospect, they may have looked askance at me. And I think they must have said something. But if they did, their words wouldn't have registered. Increasingly I was moving in a world of my own.

Despite my aspirations, however, in the days that followed, I sat for what seemed like hours in the armless rocking chair in our suite's living room. Occasionally I got up and sat in front of the bookshelf, arranging and rearranging books, unable to cease this activity, consumed with the desire to display the books just so, grouping them by binding color.

This dramatic yet silent inner life continued without anyone noticing any differences in my behavior.

Until late one night, ten days into my sophomore year.

Two in the morning. In my college dorm room. I sit silent in the suite's spindle-backed rocking chair and rock and rock and rock. I'm flying to Africa by secret plane. My MIT date from two nights ago sits next to me. We fly across the ocean to Ghana to work in a small village as two of the first volunteers for the newly formed Peace Corps. Going on a journey. My journey. I get up and fool with books on the shelf in front of me. Sit down to fly again. Get up. Arrange and rearrange the books, put them in the perfect order for the moment, decide they need more rearranging. Sit, rock, rearrange. Life is but a dream.

Three o'clock. In bed. Kick the covers off my feet and burst into song. Top of my lungs. Singing out the window down to the lake. Communing with the evergreens that line the lake. Roommates wake up, bemused, and join in. Why not? This is a hoot! "Row, row, row your boat, gently down the stream, Merrily, merrily, merrily,

merrily, life is but a dream." By the fifth verse, they're exchanging worried glances, imploring me to stop. I keep singing. They wave their arms. Stop, Marilee. They droop in frustration. One calls the dorm mother. I keep singing, communing with the trees, sending my voice out the window, across the campus lawn to the lake.

Pretty soon, the message found its way up to our suite that the college jeep was waiting outside Claflin Hall to take me to the campus infirmary. Mary Esther helped me get into my robe. I awkwardly slipped my bare feet into my loafers, and the housemother gently but firmly led me out and into the elevator. Nancy handed me a bag of clothes and a toothbrush. I must have been moving like a zombie by then.

This is it—the journey . . . I'm going, going on a journey, I said to myself.

I floated down through the building on the housemother's arm in the antiquated elevator, clutching my small bag, and rode in the college jeep to the infirmary. Once there, I lay flat on a bed in a room with a banana tree painted in its corner and hallucinated for a day or two or three more. My body felt wooden. In my unthreading mind, I anticipated the trip with Jon of MIT. It played out like a movie in my head while I lay silent and psychotic in a Wellesley infirmary bed late that September of 1961. I don't remember my exact feelings from that time, if I was even having feelings, but the mental diversion must have given me enormous comfort and focus. Little did I know the real destination of the trip I would be taking.

My mother flew in from New Orleans, leaving my four youngest siblings at home with Crutcher, Ruth, and various babysitters. My sister Penny was away at boarding school, and Pixie had begun her freshman year at Smith. In the taxi to McLean Hospital, Mom perched silently on the edge of the seat beside me in her black-and-white-checked, short-sleeved dress, stiff and doll-like. Her hands clutched her purse, her face petrified, stricken, hurt. Wind was blowing up through a twelve-inch round hole in the floor—a hole I hallucinated—and I breathed in the acrid smell of tires on asphalt, partially cloaked by Mother's floral *eau de cologne*. The driver picked up the pace. Trees whizzed by, and cars galloped down the road. I fixed my sight on the unkempt, hairy back of the driver's neck. I was a stuffed, lumpy doll.

At McLean, on lovely grounds that looked more like a college campus than a loony bin, I worked with kind doctors, social workers, and aides, and hung around, once I dared, with other patients. The ward doctor displayed compassionate acuity when he grasped that I had weighing-in and food problems. He left orders that a jar of peanut better be available to me around the clock in the corner cupboard of the dining room—a gesture that spoke volumes to me, as it connected me to Ruth's sneaking peanut butter for me under the dining room table when I was six and Daddy still lived with us, and accelerated my trust level with the staff. I also got to paint and write there, if you could call it that—my notebooks were indecipherable for a long time. And Tom Snedeker—a friend I had met at a Mardi Gras mixer at Harvard during my freshman year at Wellesley, when Tom was a senior at Hebron Academy in Maine—came to visit, but neither he, my roommates, nor most family members were allowed to see me that fall. Even though the doctors knew I'd been on Dexedrine and thyroid pills for almost ten years, no one realized until years later that I had quit them cold turkey. Maybe if the doctors had known that fact, I would have spent less time in my psychotherapist's office smelling his rich pipe tobacco.

"Stand on your own two feet, Marilee. Stand on your own two feet." Crutcher's voice reverberated in my head. I stood against the wall in McLean Hospital watching television in the living room, I stood at the dining table for meals, I stood in my room except at bedtime.

"Stand on your own two feet, Marilee." I stood to pee. The urine soaked through my panties, ran down my inner thighs, knees, and calves, dripped off my ankles, and splattered on the floor tiles.

And I wore piles and piles of clothes for my daily visits to see the psychotherapist. I can't tell you what the garments were, yet they all acted as layers of protection, layers that had to be stripped away before anyone reached me, Marilee. For the first two months I didn't utter a word. I didn't know I was psychotic, or even what that meant.

In early spring, just as I was finding my footing, I received the phone call from my mother summoning me home to become a deb and the queen of a Mardi Gras ball. I think I spent more than one session talking to my psychotherapist about how worried and conflicted I felt, about balancing my wellness with family and long-held traditions.

Chapter 5

ROYAL WHIRLWIND

I was discharged from McLean in early June 1962 and ambivalently moved into an apartment in Cambridge near Harvard Square. After my mother's summons in late spring of that year, I had spoken with my Wellesley dean, who'd said I could either wait a year to return to college or attend as a part-time student to accommodate my daily psychotherapy schedule. Annoyed and impatient, I decided to attend Boston University that September instead, where I could carry the minimum full-class load and drive weekdays to meet with my pipe-holding therapist at McLean.

Also, I had to factor in the many trips home to New Orleans I would have to make that year as a 1962–1963 debutante. Over the Thanksgiving holiday, I would fly home and be presented to society at both the Debutante Club and the newer *Le Debut des Jeunes Filles* at Thanksgiving. Besides being Queen of the Osiris Ball, I would be participating as a "maid" in balls with lofty names such as the Twelfth Night Revelers Ball, the Mithras Ball, the Momus Ball, and the Proteus Ball—all organized by krewes to which at least one of my family members belonged.

The first time I tried to light the oven in my Cambridge apartment that summer, having no clue what I was doing, I survived a small gas explosion. I felt traumatized and—after sitting numbly for a minute, eyebrows singed, face stinging, nerves jangling, unnerved, and uncertain what to do—I gathered myself and made a call and then walked five blocks to the campus infirmary to get help. After that, things settled down, although I stayed away from the oven. Since classes at Boston University wouldn't start until September, I fell into a routine of attending Harvard extension lit classes, driving to McLean for my daily mandatory therapy sessions, and walking past the Peabody Museum to Harvard Square to buy food and supplies for myself. As the days passed, I grew in the realization that I could function out of the hospital. In July, a former boarding school roommate moved in with me. I had been anticipating her arrival, excited about rekindling our friendship, but right away she started bringing home her horny boyfriend. I was flummoxed. I'd envisioned having a friend around. But she had no time for me, and I took to doing anything to avoid witnessing her affair.

Living with her was so draining, it was a relief when Mom telephoned in August, a few days before the first of my planned trips home to prepare for my roles as deb and queen. "Marilee," she said, her voice excited and proud, "your picture will be taken on Thursday for *The Times-Picayune* with a group of other debs. And on Friday, Saturday, and Monday, you'll meet with a former queen for scepter and curtsy training to prepare you for your reign in January."

I tried to say something, like *Stop!*, but she didn't pause to ask my opinion or to see if I was up for it.

"Oh, and there's a Debutante Club meeting when you return for your next trip in November. You'll meet other debs who've been invited to be in the club this year, and a few from earlier years."

I took in this information, agog and apprehensive at the coming change of pace, from slow, sheltered, regularly scheduled days at McLean to dressing for and participating in krewes' balls with dance music, bright lights, colorful costumes, ball gowns, and revelry. I hadn't been out of the routine of McLean for more than a few weeks, and I was finally getting used to the routine of living on my own. How would I fare in this whirlwind of activity?

I arrived in New Orleans from Boston in August, just in time to step into my spot in the group photo for the *Picayune*. I quickly took my place and smiled into the camera, wearing the sky-blue dress with its drapey, ill-fitting neckline that Mom thought was attractive and that we had bought during the two hours after I deplaned and we'd picked up my brothers and their friends from school and sports. We hadn't had time to have the dress fitted to me. What a shock when the photographer walked away and the group dispersed, and I realized all the other girls in the group photo were wearing white. Mom apologized to me later for the gaffe, saying she hadn't realized that the dress protocol for the newspaper photo was white. At the time, I bit my lip, feeling out of place and embarrassed. Thinking back, perhaps I should have been thankful that my mother didn't have time to pay attention to every detail. It's quite possible she suffered more than I did over my standing out in a blue, ill-fitting dress, but she never let on.

One evening during the first weekend I was home, Mom invited a few friends to the house to see me, and it all seemed quite pleasant at first—local summer chitchat, do you knows, and tinkling laughter all liquefied by a sangria concoction. One guest made a joke about his therapist, and I latched on to him. "Therapy" was a word we had in common. So when he asked me about my year, I mentioned my own therapy and my stay at McLean. Since the hospital was associated with Harvard, and he was a recent Harvard graduate, he knew of it, and we started talking with passion about psychological matters. The next thing I knew, Mom was next to me squeezing my arm, pulling me off to one side. "Shhh, don't talk about that."

I winced. *Why not talk about it? Is she embarrassed about my hospital stay? Not a topic for social conversation? This is my life, for heaven's sake.* I felt anger, then rejection, and finally hurt. Why did I still need to lie and play a role? Fit in to someone else's picture? Being myself didn't seem to be an option, and it was killing me. What good did that do?

Looking back, I see that was the central challenge for me—whether to allow myself to be me or to cover up real feelings in a way that would eventually kill me. Was she being protective? I felt marginalized before I'd even settled in. How could I not refer to my recent life? I then moved to the other end of the sofa, in too much discomfort to mingle. After a few minutes, my new *sympatico* friend made his way over and sat next to me. "We could gossip about everyone here instead of talking about our own experiences," he said, and chuckled kindly. "It'll get easier, don't you worry. Come on, let's join the others and play the game."

Mom and Crutcher had done a lot to head me in the "right" direction, but their lives were so busy that we didn't spend time talking about my having been hospitalized for nine months. The subject was avoided. Although it seemed odd to dive into a debut season on the heels of seclusion in a psych hospital, Mom thought it would be just the ticket to get me back in the groove. And when she wanted something, she often got it.

It was a punishing schedule, even in those first couple of weeks at home in August. And then Mom showed me the calendar for the next five visits home. Thanksgiving weekend: Wednesday night the Bachelor Club Party, Thursday family Thanksgiving, Friday night presentation at *Le Debut des Jeunes*

Filles de la Nouvelle Orleans, and Saturday the Debutante Club presentation. Then at Christmas, other debs' parties, my grandparents' New Year's Eve debut party for Malcie and me, and the first ball of the Carnival season, Twelfth Night Revelers Ball. I would return to be Queen of Osiris at the end of January, and on a subsequent trip appear in the balls of Mithras, Momus, Mystick, and Proteus. Even then I suspected that it would be an anticlimax to come back and be a maid after I'd been a queen, but on the other hand, I could relax and have more fun.

I took a breath and reeled back on my heels. I felt as if someone were holding a wet washcloth over my face when I thought of returning home five more times that year for parties and balls. What had I gotten myself into? I knew Mom thought this debut year would bring me back to being a normal girl, but I still wondered. Should I reconsider? Standing there, I felt sick and shaky, but as usual, I said nothing.

The deb presentations in the fall rolled into the New Orleans Carnival or Mardi Gras season and became intertwined. The season opens on the sixth of January when the Twelfth Night Revelers host their ball—on the twelfth night of Christmas. It lasts until Mardi Gras day, forty-seven days before Easter. So Mardi Gras can fall anywhere from early February to early March, depending on Easter's date, which changes according to the phases of the moon.

The tight August schedule continued after the embarrassing group deb photo. My mom had agreed that I could fly to Dallas with my stepmother, Hettie, to select ball gowns at Neiman Marcus between scepter lessons. She almost pushed me out the door. That was surprising, since she was relinquishing her role as my clothes selector, a role she was really good at and one that was essential to my coming out as a deb and playing the role of the queen. Maybe she pushed me out of the way so she could take care of the other children. All I know is that she expected me to fulfill the deb and queen role without her help in selecting my wardrobe.

On the way to the airport, Hettie said, "I'm friendly with a saleslady at Neiman's who helps me pick out career clothes and ball gowns." Hettie was an executive at Avondale Shipyards and had many outfits for the part. "You must be excited to be home again and about to make your debut."

I nodded my head and said I was glad, but I didn't tell her that I felt uncomfortable being with her—I'd probably never had a real conversation with her that wasn't about my dad or what I wanted for Christmas and birthday presents. What would we talk about? The huge vessels her company was building on the edge of the Mississippi? The ranch she'd grown up on in Texas? How she had fallen in love with my father? I was much more at ease with my mother, who knew intuitively which clothes were good on me. Hettie worked as an executive in a large shipbuilding company. As a career woman, she was more buttoned up about outfits—hats, gloves, shoes, purses to match. I worried that Mom might not like my Texas selections. We got out of the taxi and looked up at the building that housed this upscale retail store.

"Come on, Marilee, let's have some fun," Hettie said. "I'm thrilled we're here, and I want to see you pick out three ball dresses that please you. You'll be wearing them often in the coming months."

I relaxed a little. Her light-toned guidance was reassuring. Not uptight. We proceeded into the store and walked straight past the jewelry and handbag counters up the escalator to the ball dress department. Hettie was my cheerleader while I tried on a dozen pretty long dresses. I wound up selecting one long shamrock-green sleeveless, scoop neck dress and two white ones—one very formal with a scoop neck bordered with fine bugle beading that I would wear for the big *Le Debut* event on

Thanksgiving weekend when Daddy was to be my escort. I liked the dresses so much that I forgot to worry about whether my mother would like them. I was happily excited and also grabbed three purses I liked, two pairs of shoes, and two pairs of long kidskin gloves. I was having fun and couldn't stop smiling. Hettie turned out to be relaxed and fun on this trip, letting me make my own selections with the neutral help of the saleswoman. It felt freeing not to be deferring to Mom's ideas.

Selecting the dresses I would wear to the balls made me excited about being part of the deb and Mardi Gras seasons that built up to the Mardi Gras parades. I remembered how happy I'd been as a child at the parades.

One of my favorite photos shows me as a little girl on Mardi Gras day with my father, mother, and my sister Pixie. She and I were ages three and four, wearing loosely fitted blue clown outfits with huge cotton gauze pompoms and neck ruffs over sweaters, arriving in front of some friends' house on St. Charles Avenue, the main thoroughfare through Uptown New Orleans, where the Rex parade would soon roll by on its way to people-packed Canal Street. Over her left arm, Mom carried a shoulder bag with her lipstick and other essentials tucked inside. Live oak trees lined the avenue. Shiny aspidistras rippled in the breeze in the spaces between sidewalk and street. We looked like a happy and excited family, ready for the Carnival festivities, about to meet up with friends.

The distant drumbeat of the Carnival parade's marching bands resonated in my young body that day and made an imprint—Mardi Gras was already running in my blood. When I heard the trombones and trumpets in the distance, I danced and moved around like everyone around me, throwing one hip this way, the other one that way, while holding hands with my parents.

Through the years, I always anticipated parade season. It provided a great excuse to talk to anyone you saw on the street.

Out on the parade route, I was always amazed that the tractor drivers pulling the floats managed to avoid the crowds
and particularly the children in the street. Black men carrying
flambeaux or torches flanked the night parades and wore low-
slung leather belts equipped with a leather pocket in front that
anchored a pole topped by burning cloth and oil fuel. They provided the light that showed off the floats.

At the passing of each float you'd hear "Throw me some-
thin', mistuh!" reverberating in the crowd. Kids and adults
wrangled for the dozens and dozens of shiny beads and dou-
bloons minted for the various krewes and thrown by masked
men from the floats which towered ten to fifteen feet above the
streets. Even as an adult, my pulse would speed up. My body is
imprinted with the practiced motion of elbowing my way to a
good position to catch throws, especially if I thought I knew the
masker on the float.

When that first visit home ended, I must have been still
whirling from the social schedule, because I hardly remember
the flight back to Boston in time for the start of my classes at
Boston University. I moved into my own new tiny apartment
with a two-burner stove overlooking Boylston Street between
Harvard Square and the Charles River. Each day I drove my
family's 1954 green Plymouth—delivered from New Orleans
by the family handyman—from my apartment to BU on Commonwealth Avenue in Boston, and to therapy at McLean in
Belmont.

Soon it was time to go south again. I flew home the day
before Thanksgiving, and that night found myself adjusting
the shoulder strap of my long white scoop neck dress, with
its elegant bands of silk ruching, just before participating in
the debutante presentation of the Bachelors' Club. Mom had
told me the club had been founded in 1934 as a place where
young men and women of similar backgrounds could meet and

socialize. Later I learned it was run by a committee of older men who selected the new debutantes to be presented each year. Or rather, selected the fathers and male guardians whose daughters would be presented. You could say it was the male gateway to a debutante's year. I heard that a man who was affluent but not considered suitable would be passed over by the committee; they picked only upper echelon members. I don't know if prospective members applied for selection or simply had to stand by to see if they were invited.

Apparently, the primary function of the club was to put on a social ritual where forty to fifty new debutantes, wearing white and holding the arms of their fathers or guardians, would be presented to society—to club members, family, and friends— and then to host the dance that followed. A year before I was presented, a newer organization had started, *Le Debut des Jeunes Filles de la Nouvelle Orleans*, not a replacement for the Debu- tante Club but an organization that operated concurrently. It had been formed with the idea of eliminating the requirement of the Debutante Club for a deb to have multiple parties given for her by parents and others—the new idea, as I remember, was that families could get together to host events, thus eliminating some of the expense, and to reduce the number of events that debs and their families had to attend. A step toward enlighten- ment! Of course, my family enrolled me in both, as they didn't know which would become the more important group to the deb season, and I had three sisters presumably coming after me.

At the Bachelors' Club, dressed in white, standing beside an escort in white tails who chatted without pause with what seemed like an exaggerated Southern accent and manners, I felt ill at ease, weird, out of place. My mother had arranged our date from a list of eligible bachelors, and I was mortified at the thought of spending the evening with whomever he was. I looked around for some of my female peers, also dressed in white and holding the arms of escorts in early stages of inebriation. In the end, I did everything I was supposed to do to be part of my tribe, including drinking, marching around the room, smiling, and interacting with others. "And what fraternity are you in? You're from St. Joe? Cousins in Natchez? Yes, I go to Biloxi in the summer." But really, part of me was absent. The Bachelors' Club presentation of the debs was awkward, but nothing compared to what was to come.

I had hoped the next event, the Saturday night cotillion, *Le Debut des Jeunes Filles de la Nouvelle Orleans*, would be an improvement over the Bachelors' Club party. But the morning after Thanksgiving, my mother took me aside and dashed those hopes. "Marilee, plans have changed. Crutcher is going to escort you Saturday night at *Le Debut*, not your father. You'll have to tell your father."

I felt sick. What the hell was she thinking? Why was she pushing me into an untenable situation? "Mom, no. How could you do this to Daddy? He's my father. Of course he's going to escort me. His friends expect him to escort me, and he expects to escort me. That would be so unfair. And at the last minute like this. That is cruel. Screwed up."

Mom was oddly silent, and I quickly realized the probable crux of the matter. Crutcher was paying for my presentation, not my dad. And Mom hadn't had the courage to say anything out loud to him, to me, or to Daddy. I fumed. I wondered how the conversation had gone between Crutcher and Mom when they discussed this matter. Or had it even been discussed? I felt upset, but I agreed to break the news to Daddy and Hettie—I knew there was no way Mom would tell him. Years later, I recalled the inability of both of my parents to deal with what was right in front of them, how the presentation would be handled.

I dreaded the task, but I got into a car and drove up St. Charles to the Carrollton section where Hettie and Daddy lived.

I walked up the steps and rang the bell, a lump in my throat, willing myself to be on automatic pilot. Both of them answered the door, surprised and delighted to see me. I hugged each awkwardly and got right to it.

"Mom said to tell you that Crutcher is going to escort me Saturday night at *Le Debut.*" I said it staccato, loud, defensive, my body trembling, the lining behind my eyes tight. This *is not my problem*, I said to myself, but I hated my predicament.

"What?" Hettie shrieked, her hand over her heart.

Daddy looked like a deer in the headlights.

Warrior and protector of Daddy, Hettie drew herself up to her full height of five feet ten inches, looked at me, and said, "Crutcher is behind this, Marilee. You have to stand up to him."

I looked her straight in the eye and said, "This is between my mother and my father. It is not my problem, and I refuse to allow this to ruin my weekend." I surprised myself, coolly suppressing my deepest fear that that I might fall apart over this squabble because I felt guilty, of course. After all, she and I had had such fun shopping at Neiman's together for the dress I would be wearing at the event.

Daddy was silent. Hettie fumed. I didn't stay for a Coke.

Saturday night, *Le Debut* rolled around. I was one of four dozen girls my age dressed in the requisite long white gowns and white kid gloves reaching just above our elbows, carrying bouquets of red roses in our arms, crowned by hairdos so full of spray that no strand of hair could stray. There's a photo of me smiling, wearing the dress with the delicate bugle beading that I had chosen with Hettie and she had bought, standing next to Crutcher, my mother, my grandmother Nainnain, an uncle, and my debutante cousin Malcie of attic crown-and-scepter mischief, also in white, just outside the entrance to the presentation hall. No Daddy.

A master of ceremonies announced the names of each debutante and of our parents. When it was my turn, Crutcher escorted me across a wide dance floor covered with white canvas. I danced the two-step with him to the tune, *'S Wonderful*, armpits sweaty, feeling guilty from the tension of knowing that Daddy and Hettie were somewhere in the audience. The music of that first dance stopped, and I said to myself, *This is not something I created. It is not my problem.* But my words didn't prevent me from the pain of knowing that I had chosen to go along with my mother's demand and had disappointed my dad.

During my debutante year, in addition to being presented with other debutantes at a ball, I attended the club's annual tea for current and former debutantes. A female deb committee ran this event, the women either appointed by the men behind the scenes or made up of ladies who'd served as officers of an executive committee. Debutantes from my year were in attendance, along with those from earlier years as well, everyone dressed up in suits and dresses for this teatime ritual.

After the tea it was back to Boston University, English and government classes, and I don't remember what else. As fun as some of the socializing had been, it was a great relief to return to my own cozy apartment and the routine of attending classes on Commonwealth Avenue and driving to McLean, studying, doing laundry in the basement, putting meals together, anonymity.

Why didn't I quit the debut right then? My sense of loyalty and obligation to the ritual, to parents and grandparents overruled any desultory thoughts I might have had about bailing out. Not to mention how long I had waited for this. As usual, my feelings flip-flopped. And after all, a custom-made queen's dress was being constructed and beaded for me. So much was at stake. I was also beginning to realize that I was having some fun. It became increasingly easy to go along with the program. I didn't yet have the clarity or the tools that would have helped me stand up to my social peers. I was just beginning to wake up to the larger parts of myself.

Chapter 6

QUEEN OF THE BALL

The Christmas holidays snuck up quickly, crammed with obligations, including additional dress fittings and scepter training for my role as queen. The Osiris Ball was only a month away. I took lessons from a former queen on the correct way to carry sixty pounds of beaded dress and collared harness and eighty pounds of ermine-trimmed velvet train behind me. She taught me how to conduct myself during the Grand March—how to wave the scepter, to circle the open ballroom ceremonially, to bow to mothers and grandmothers and guests, and to march around again with the king, leading all the maids in the court and their escorts back to their stations in the grand tableau. Very exacting instructions for what I was to do in the ceremonial Grand March.

On Christmas Eve, I attended Nainnain and E.O.'s dinner dance at the elegant old Roosevelt Hotel for me and my cousin Malcie; we'd come a long way since finding the crown and scepter in the attic. I had such a high-spirited time in my new shamrock-green dress from Neiman's until my date—the one with the background in psychological matters—said something that extinguished my good mood at the end of a dance by announcing that he was falling in love with another debutante. She would subsequently reign as Queen of Rex, not that we were privy to that secret at the time. The Queen of Rex holds a special place, since Rex and his consort are in effect the king and queen of all Carnival. The photos of both monarchs were displayed on Mardi Gras day on the front page of the *Times-Picayune* with long articles about their royal selves and their lineages. Who was the Queen of Osiris in relation to her?

I was getting into the swing of things. I woke up at noon and guzzled down café au lait, checked my date book for appointments, washed and set my hair, talked with girlfriends on the phone or met them in the park. But something was missing, and the new beauty rituals and the fuss acted as a foil against allowing that nagging something to come to consciousness. In the meantime, the ball given by the Twelfth Night Revelers captured my fancy.

The old-line balls that I knew about were run by white men in elite social organizations. A small number of men kept a tight grip on the makeup of the Mardi Gras krewes through the selection of officers, including the krewe captain, the king and queen who were chosen to represent the krewe publicly, and the debutante court maids. Even though Mardi Gras had been recognized as a festivity since before the Civil War, the introduction of royalty roles, along with presentations of daughters of krewe members—the debutantes named as court maids—began in 1872 at the Twelfth Night Revelers Ball. Years later I mulled over the thought that the men organizing the balls slotted the women in this class for maids and queens, as if to honor the women, but it looked as if they were enthralling them, by placing them on a pedestal, into accepting a system that honored the supremacy of white men. So much for male gallantry.

Starting in the 1930s, the krewes transformed the interior spaces of the multipurpose Municipal Auditorium near the French Quarter into lavish and elegant throne settings fit for royalty. From the thrones, the monarchs waved their scepters to two classes of guests—those invited to participate or dance in the Maskers' Ball on the main floor, and those in the balcony provided for non-call-out guests invited to watch the spectacle from a level above. Some of these old-line krewes put on parades with floats. Secrecy was a key ingredient, symbolized by the wearing of costumes and disguises, the hierarchy of invitations, the identity of the kings, and the behind-the-scenes plotting that went on year in and year out to determine who would be queen the following year and the year after that.

The Twelfth Night Revelers Ball was not only full of this pomp and pageantry, it also provided a setting where I felt comfortable in my tribe. I wore the *de rigueur* white dress—another dress from Neiman's, this one strapless with embossed circles as big as plates. I knew that both my father's and my mother's male relatives were involved in this krewe, so I harbored the expectation that I might be selected for the court, but the adults in the know wouldn't reveal the identity of the court until the night at the ball. The suspense gave me fits.

Dominating the stage at the ball was a large white king's cake. Dozens of tiny boxes with pieces of the king's cake and a ball favor were being offered to all the young maiden women called out on the dance floor, and a certain number of boxes containing silver beans inside the cake were given to those debs selected as court maids. I felt delight and relief when I opened my box to find a silver kidney-shaped bean pendant on a long chain. I was a maid! We applauded the tall, dark-haired, slender young woman, cheeks bright red, who pulled the gold bean, the queen's bean, from the cake. She almost fainted with surprise. As court maids, we lined up with our masked escorts and, conversing politely, excitedly, and sometimes elegantly, participated in a short Grand March. Then we danced with our maskers. By my early dream's standards, I had arrived. I went home content after being a maid in my first Carnival ball and packed for the trip back to Boston.

In late January I flew down south for the fourth of my five debut-year trips home. During that trip I went to my last scepter lesson, joked with the seamstress at a fitting for my elaborate queen's dress, and rehearsed for the Grand March for the Osiris Ball. The moment I'd dreamed about as a girl in the attic was at hand. My friend Helen Scott from Boston, a tall, lanky blonde, joined me as a guest for the weekend. Older sister to one of my friends, she'd taken me under her wing weekends at her Beacon Hill apartment during my last couple months at McLean. Once a debutante herself in Richmond, Virginia, she expressed wide-eyed curiosity for our Carnival season filled with royalty and elaborately decorated floats and ball tableaux and masked dancers.

Over the last few trips, I'd had numerous fittings for my heavily beaded paisley-patterned gown at Town & Country Dress Shop, headquarters for queens' dresses for decades. On the day of the ball, I entered the shop excitedly with my entourage—Mom, Helen, and Ruth shepherding my little sister and brothers. Em Walker, the shop proprietor, and Mrs. Royal, her petite chief dressmaker, acted as my support team and encouraged me all the way. They helped me step into an elaborately constructed metal corset and collar, made intricate adjustments, and then invited me to put on my beaded dress.

"Yikes," I cried out. "I feel as if I'm in a torture chamber," and laughed with everyone else. I was five feet five inches and 155 pounds—all that peanut butter at McLean—heavy by my standards, but the dress was so cinched in at my waist that I felt I looked pretty good. I glanced at my mother in her ball gown and imagined that she was wishing I had shed twenty pounds before the ball.

At that point, the barrel-chested hair stylist to debutantes par excellence, always dressed in a suit and tie, full-figured and dignified, stepped in to take control of my hair, securing the rhinestone crown to my head with a hundred bobby pins, talking to me the whole time. He chuckled as he recited the important reasons for making a debut.

"You learn manners that will always serve you. You hold your place in society. And you meet eligible men."

Helen chimed in and said, "I can't think of any other city in the country that treats their debutantes so royally."

"Oh, yes," the seamstress said, "the city of Mobile. They're older than we are here."

As he patted a curl into place, the stylist winked at the shop owner and said, "Our elegant and good-humored shop proprietress and unassuming socialite will agree with me. You are playing a role in a long and glamorous history tonight. I feel honored to be serving your majesty."

I said, "Go on. You've been fixing my hair for parties all year, and thank heavens you are doing it now." I looked in the mirror for the tenth time. "I do look different, don't I?" The fact was, I was caught up in the rituals of Mardi Gras and enjoyed the attention I was receiving, even if the only reason I was there was to honor my grandfather. I liked the bright shiny colors, the music on the streets and at the balls. I liked dressing up as a queen.

At the dress shop, as I checked myself out in the mirror in my queen's dress, Em Walker, who stood five feet eleven inches tall, her form curved in a slender S, handed me a glass of champagne. Coincidentally, she and I were both graduates of St. Timothy's School, fifty years apart, and she had been a queen of both Rex and Comus in the early 1920s. Raising her glass, she said, smiling, "To a regal and beautiful queen," her elfish eyes and dimples grinning. "You look beautiful. I knew you would. You'll knock 'em dead." I was toasted amid friendly laughter, and it helped me relax.

There's a photo that I cherish—I in my queen's dress standing next to our cook and babysitter, Ruth, in her best starched and ironed uniform. She had come to the shop with her charges, my younger siblings—eleven-year-old sister Allison, who was all eyes, and my younger brothers Bruce, nine, and John, seven— playing around on the floor, cutting up. Years later, I'd realize that by posing in my queen's gown with Ruth in her uniform, proud as she appeared to be in the picture with me, I had fostered the ancient etiquette that kept black and white races in the places preferred by descendants of plantation owners. Things were less transparent in my day in my circles. I was pretty much oblivious to racial inequality. I sensed an oddness in my chest—a flutter that something unnamed was not right—but couldn't see it to name it.

Thinking of the number of people involved in creating my queen's dress, I am amazed at the substantial industry that Mardi Gras engenders—musicians, dressmakers, dress shops, krewe members, dry cleaners, shoe shops, caterers, maids, bartenders, bands, bead shops, restaurants, liquor distributors, artists, designers, printers, painters, tractor mechanics and drivers, flambeaux carriers, firemen, cooks, policemen, sanitation crews, babysitters, jewelers, florists, and street vendors. Further, extensive and profitable business opportunities sprang from social Carnival connections made across the city. The economy of New Orleans, then run by the white business leaders and captains of men's krewes, might just collapse if Mardi Gras ceased to exist. My family during my deb year contributed greatly to the city's commerce and financial well-being, that is for sure.

The night of the ball, dress and crown in place, I entered the limousine and rode with my mother and the women from the shop to the auditorium. At last we were on our way!

My grandfather, E.O., blue eyes sparkling, dressed in tails and white tie, stood at the entrance waiting for us. My heart fluttered with excitement seeing him there. Ducking my broad rhinestone collar, he gave my gloved arm a squeeze and pecked me on the cheek.

Years later, I found letters from my stepfather to my king and to the captain of the ball, thanking them for the honor of having me as queen, assuring them that I'd had a wonderful time and that I so appreciated how smoothly everything had gone. I was touched by his note, by this sign of his participation. The year I was queen, I wrote my own thank-you notes to the captain who had invited me to be queen, to the king who had presented me with a watch. I also sent dozens of other notes that year to thank hostesses for parties and friends for presents. Performing a family duty was part of the experience of being a queen, but that duty wasn't on my mind as I prepared for my role. I wasn't thinking about the significant status and public honor given to the family of a queen. I was thinking about whether I was waving my scepter correctly, if my hair looked all right under the crown, and whether I could pull off moving the heavy train around the floor. And who would I know at this ball?

After my grandfather welcomed me, the shop ladies attached the Osiris organization's long, ermine-trimmed, eighty-pound train to my Medici-style collar. Feeling the restriction of the corset I wore, I thought of those cultures that bind young girls' feet. I was equipped with a stiff hairdo, crown, strong corset, ornate dress, and scepter—fulfilling that dream first hatched in E.O.'s attic. It was time for the ball to begin. My dressing team walked me to the appointed entry place. Mom in her magenta ball gown sat in her front-row seat with my grandmother, my aunt, and Helen Scott. Crutcher—wearing a sateen costume and mask—mingled in the crowd of krewe members. My king was a prominent doctor and rancher and father of one of my classmates. Feeling excited and nervous, we made our grand entrance into the larger side of the ball space at the Municipal Auditorium and waved our scepters to all the guests, those seated on the ground floor and those in the balcony! After a march around the ballroom, again waving our scepters in unison, we proceeded up the shallow and deep white-canvassed steps to our gilded thrones, exchanged a nod to each other, turned slowly to accommodate the weight of our ermine-tail-trimmed trains aided by two pairs of pages, and faced the U-shaped configuration of theater chairs and the balcony above, wielding our scepters slowly in greeting. After more curtseying from the court, trumpets announced the Grand March. First the king was escorted down the steps to the floor on one side, then I followed, escorted to the spot next to him, both of us, again, holding our scepters. The ritual of it!

The king turned toward me and said, "Marilee, are you ready?"

I smiled back at him, my stomach fluttering, but appreciating his kind words.

Physically, I struggled to haul the weight of the ermine train behind me. The king and I walked ceremonially around the huge ballroom, chatting in small snippets to stay animated. When we processed near my mother's seat, I said, "Here are my mom and grandmother."

I looked Mom in the eye, held the king's hand and, lowering my head, torso, and thighs, back straight, made a queenly curtsey to her, and then curtsied to Nain.

We circled the room again and returned to our thrones, always followed ceremonially by the court maids and their escorts. At this point, I sighed with relief, knowing the attention would now shift away from us and on to the court maids. It was time for them to dance with the krewe's maskers. Once that was completed, young women as well as older matrons would be called onto the floor to dance by the Krewe of Osiris maskers. The king and I remained seated stiffly on our thrones as we greeted guests who made the trek across the dance floor to bow or curtsey and say hello. No dancing for us. I liked waving my scepter. I was doing my job! I flashed back to my grandparents' attic. In fact, at that moment I felt I had been born to do this. I was wrapped up in my role and didn't give a thought to my earlier hesitations about exactly what I was doing. And the dancing continued to the cheerful and familiar music of René Louapre's Society Orchestra.

At the queen's supper following the ball, borrowed ermine train thankfully returned to the care of the Osiris organization, the words of my Richmond-born houseguest stunned me. "This is unbelievable," she said. "Absolutely unbelievable. It's so bizarre." She rolled her eyes, laughing. "This is so much ritual based on royalty and magical thinking."

My gut felt hollow. Was there something to what she said? It nagged at me. Was there some truth to it? I think some part of me had questioned this whole process, but her words—*unbelievable, bizarre*—rang in my head until I had to put them aside. I would carry away with me the incredulous look on her face when she made these comments. She and her sister had been debutantes in Richmond, but that was a simple cotillion affair— young women being introduced to society with no royalty involved. Kings and queens wielding scepters, a gaggle of maids and princesses following after us, the seated guests standing and clapping in response, the call-out tradition, the earnest tenor of the whole affair—her comments popped my own eyes open and gave rise to my first inkling that our Mardi Gras traditions in New Orleans were not only considered singular by many but were in fact rather odd, to say the least.

I went to bed at five in the morning, my body aching from pulling the eighty-pound train of my gown around the floor but content that I had done a good job as queen. I'd had multiple misgivings about making my debut, but I was enjoying this now.

Back and forth, back and forth. Boston for two weeks, then time for another plane to New Orleans, where I paraded—as a maid this time, not a queen—across the white canvas floor at the Momus Ball wearing my favorite white dress with the white satin dots, on the arm of one of the young masked dukes. My dad, masked and costumed, sat cross-legged on the floor of the ballroom alongside other masked krewe members, holding his cotton favor bag full of small gifts for anyone he would dance with. As weird as it was to see those seated men clapping their white cotton-gloved hands, it energized me, and I nearly bounded across the floor to them.

"Nornie, Nornie, Nornie," they called amid catcalls and whistles. "Nornie, Nornie, Nornie."

I marched, back straight, proud, grinning, thrilled to hear my dad's name shouted out, grasping how beloved he was by this group of men. In these moments, Momus felt like family. One of my nieces, a recent debutante and queen, summed up her deb experience in my daughter Rebecca's documentary when she said, "It's nice to be fussed over." That was true for me, too. But those moments at the Momus Ball, when I felt like I belonged, that I was beautiful and valued and seen, were more important to me. I may not have always thought like those men and women did, but you could say that these were my people. Or rather, my dad's people.

I played the role of a maid in one more ball the night before Mardi Gras day, the Proteus Ball, wearing my bugle bead dress one last time. It was kind of a ho-hum ending after a full season, although Proteus's underwater tableau setting was my favorite. My suitcases were already packed for Boston when I danced among the masked crowd. The next morning, Mardi Gras day, while the parades were rolling and most everyone I knew was dancing in the streets watching Zulu and Rex and the truck parades ride by, I threw my bags into a taxi to the airport to fly back to Boston, relieved to be on my way back to my own life. I walked into the main concourse, looked around at the clean parabola curve of the vast roof built in 1960, and saw people dressed in everyday suits and jeans, carrying on business that had nothing to do with the scene I had just left behind. How dreary and colorless seemed this space and how bright and colorful the world I had just left.

As I walked to my gate, I looked up at a small TV screen blasting the news. My jaw dropped. *O Lord!* There on the screen was the image of my grandfather, E.O., dressed in top hat and morning coat. He stood next to Rex's float that had braked on Canal Street by the Boston Club, one hand holding onto a step-ladder in front of the Boston Club, the other hand clutching a glass of champagne. I heard him shout out a toast to the king on the float, "Hail Rex, Hail Rex, Hail Rex."

I gawked, riveted, and watched E.O. turn and raise his glass to my grandmother, who sat in the second row of the queen's stand. I teared up, glued to the spot. The scene on the TV seemed like a page from a storybook. I glanced around and noticed the worn scuffmarks on the terminal floor. My eyes returned to the screen showing the parade passing by the Boston Club for a minute after my grandfather stepped off the ladder. To watch the fairy-tale world of royalty on TV while waiting to fly off to my life of classes and therapy sessions in Boston was freakish, surreal, unearthly in this between-the-worlds place.

I had spent a year of moving in and out of this fantastical, secretive, exclusionary world that I had come from, a world that drove much of New Orleans' economy—and now I was leaving it, headed to straitlaced Boston, to figure out who I was and how to live in the world, not a fairy-tale kingdom of kings and queens. To do that I'd have to leave that world behind, undo the ties that bind. I allowed myself to feel the deep sense of grief in my chest at my loss of innocence and never being able to be at home in that world anymore. I took another breath and gathered myself to continue on.

Chapter 7

My Baron

In June 1963, having just finished my sophomore year, I stood dwarfed next to the Italian freighter that would carry me across the Atlantic from Brownsville, Texas, to Genoa, Italy. I was twenty-one and had recently left the whirlwind of Mardi Gras royalty behind only a few months earlier. I was nervous and excited about this voyage to new places.

At supper in Brownsville earlier that day, I sat next to my father, who was fingering a glass of bourbon with one hand and holding a lighted cigarette in the other. While he swapped stories with the ship's agent, I daydreamed, wondering what in the world it would be like to live on the ship for more than two weeks by myself. I'd packed a stack of books—including one for learning Italian—yarn to knit a sweater for my father, and a fresh journal, so I had plenty to keep me occupied. I'd been allowed to make this voyage alone because my father trusted the ship's captain, whom he'd known for a long time through his work greeting foreign ship captains and agents in his cotton khaki suits on the docks of New Orleans.

I holed up in my spacious cabin and read and knitted for a couple of days, studied my Italian Berlitz book, and read *Fanny Hill* more than once, emerging only for meals with the captain, the engineer, and an Italian American couple returning to Italy for the first time in fifty years. At times, I walked on the only deck accessible to me. And when I did, I became excruciatingly aware of the male crew members performing their tasks to keep the boat going. I'd been reading too much *Fanny Hill*. It was such a small world for nineteen days. Once we docked in Genoa, I took a cab to the train station and pulled my suitcase up onto the railcar heading for Rome, where I met up with two sisters from Richmond, Virginia, fellow St. Tim's graduates. Cinch was three years older than I, and her sister had been Pixie's friend and classmate. They had invited Pixie to join them on the trip, but my parents had decided it was my turn for an adventure. It was odd knowing that those two Virginia sisters had anticipated my sister Pixie's company, not mine, but once our journey began, I stopped thinking about it.

The three of us zipped around Rome, poking into one cathedral or museum after another wherever we were. By the end of August 1963, after sightseeing in Italy, France, and Spain for two months, we were ready for some quiet time and headed to southeast Austria to the baronial estate of their distant cousin Fritz. When we arrived at his home—a castle really, a *Schloss*— he welcomed us royally and took us on walks and excursions around his large, timbered property. And I thought I'd left royalty behind!

I was immediately intrigued. The twinkle in his eyes and the warm playfulness he directed toward the two sisters endeared him to me right away. When he looked at me teasingly, I felt a flutter in my groin. Maybe it was one of the effects of parading in front of my dad's friends at the balls, but I was drawn to older men who admired me. Thirteen years older, Fritz seemed attentive and charming, familiar, like some of those men I knew back home. He made intense eye contact with me, brushing his arm against mine more than once. He seemed like one of those men who was used to getting his way, though softly.

I fell for him—charming, solicitous, funny, and thoughtful. My plan to go home at the end of the summer vanished. Cinch had spent time at Fritz's *Schloss* on several earlier trips, and I thought I detected a slight ruffle of feathers from her every time Fritz paid attention to me. A week later, after three months of travel together, Cinch and her sister flew back to the States. Encouraged by Fritz, I remained at the castle, having decided to extend my stay in Austria, pending permission from my family. I wrote to Mother and Crutcher, a convincing letter with my plans to study German at the *Universitat*, then left the castle in September to travel to England to visit friends.

When I returned from England, the letter from my parents giving permission to stay had arrived. *Oh, my God, I'm staying!* I couldn't remember a time when I'd received what I wanted with such ease.

Late one snowy autumn afternoon, Fritz announced that we were in for a cold nocturnal adventure. I strapped on hiking boots, borrowed one of his warm jackets, and we took off with a couple of his friends in tow. Exhausted after two hours of uphill climbing, I was thrilled when we finally entered a forest shelter that slept twenty-four. I was told to sleep as best as I could for the next three hours. We awakened at midnight and continued our trek until Fritz gestured for us to stop talking and find a spot to sit and wait in the snow to watch for two woodcocks.

Soon I was so cold I couldn't feel my toes. I knew that at any moment I might topple into the snow-laden branches of the ash tree next to me. Surely, the much-heralded woodcocks would appear on this Styrian mountain before my legs grew numb. I was there because of Fritz. I would have gone anywhere with him. He'd repeatedly warned me not to move an inch, but after almost two hours of waiting, I was at my wits' end. By that point, it was two in the morning, and my urban white Southern rearing hadn't prepared me for being still for so long, especially in the woods, and in the cold. I focused my mind on the way Fritz had smelled during our encounter the previous night—a faint scent of Bay Rum. I pictured the rumpled cardinal-printed sheets in his guest room at the *Schloss*. I drew his wool jacket tighter around me. I was frozen and on the brink of giving up seeing the woodcocks' mountainside mating.

After an interminable wait, Fritz suddenly whispered, "There."

I followed his forefinger to a mass hopping across the snow forty feet away. Oh, my. They were here: two feathered creatures in a paced slow dance, one of them opening a fan of tail feathers. I forgot about my numb feet and gaped at the divinely choreographed movement, listening to the patterned sounds of these exquisite woodcocks outlined against the snow. It was easy to forget the arduous cold hike up the mountain, the all-too-short rest on cots in the rangers' quarters, and the difficult work of trekking in the dark. This had been worth the wait for something I never could have imagined doing or seeing back in the States. I loved these woods and this new world of being outdoors. I felt strong and happy—I was high—and thrilled with these adventures with Fritz.

During the next two months, Fritz took me into other mountain settings where he kept meticulous track of wildlife, breaking for delicious intervals of fun and passion in his isolated hunting cabins along the way. Sometimes we hiked with his friends, and he would tease me, "Your thighs are getting stronger!" And I would burn with humiliation that my thighs were not stronger, but his remarks gave me hope. This was the first time I had spent in the great outdoors other than at summer camp in Tennessee or the short time my family spent in hills and forests of western North Carolina when Mom was pregnant with Allison. Family life at the Biloxi compound was too tame to count.

During this time, I traveled to Vienna and stayed by myself in Fritz's flat to study German at the university. On my first day of class, I slid into a seat, relieved to have located the classroom, next to students from Syria, Egypt, Turkey, and Iran, fascinated to meet people from the Middle East. Immediately our tall, self-possessed instructor, a woman dressed in a handsome woolen suit, bright-eyed and comfortable in her role as maestra, announced, *"Alles sprechen Deutsch in klasse, alles sprechen Deutsch hier, bitte."* Everyone was to speak German and nothing but German in class. With three daily classes, I quickly became saturated. In fact, I delighted in learning a new language, so it was like eating candy.

On a visit that fall to the *Schloss*, Fritz drove me to the city of Graz and supervised as I ordered and paid for two dirndls to wear during my time in Austria. "One cotton for everyday and the other one silk for more formal occasions like Christmas," he said, helping me pick out my colors, acting more like an older brother than the lover he had become. So efficient! However, I felt warm all over from his admiring looks when I tried on the dirndls, and when I saw my reflection in the mirror, I was startled at how the dirndl style showed off my curves to advantage. He also took me to a boutique in Vienna where, with debut gift money from friends of my parents, I bought a street-length warm sheepskin coat, fitted at the waist.

That fall, Fritz and I ate and drank at the Heurigen with his friends, drinking green Austrian wine by the glass at tables situated under grapevines. Shopping together, having fun, teasing, and making love were punctuated sharply by desert-like periods, when I saw him less often and sometimes experienced excruciating loneliness. During this time, I learned a great deal about lying to myself, denying, as I did, my desire to see him much more often.

"Dear Marilee," he said to me as we walked into the courtyard of his *Schloss* one late fall morning, "you understand, I must spend enough time in Munich with Maja."

I vaguely knew of her existence but was not too happy to dwell on the reality of her. He'd become engaged to Maja not too long after he had divorced his first wife during the months before I first arrived at his castle with my travel companions, his cousins. Now, I thought, *And what about me, you creep?* I felt an emptiness in my gut, my protective shell subtly hardening. All the fun we'd been having, and I was only now grasping that he was engaged. Even then, I knew intuitively that for Fritz, marrying this woman would be a step up socially from the marriage from which he'd extracted himself, and that as an Austrian, he was embedded in a certain rigid system of social status—maybe more rigid even than the distinct social Mardi Gras system I had come from in New Orleans. That didn't concern me, I told myself, because I would be returning to the States within a few months.

So onward, ignore the sudden buzzing in your ears. Be independent. This was no new pattern, being on the fringe, having an adventure, and being alone. It was alright up to a point, I even knew that, and I made plans for myself so I wouldn't dwell on Fritz's absences. I attended superb performances at the Vienna Opera and standing-room-only performances at the Burgtheater, visited Schoenbrunn and the Albertina, read German novels, marveled at the patterned roof of the cathedral. I drank coffee with cream, ate tons of Wiener schnitzel and yogurt with fruit, and blissed out on *Sachertorte* in nineteenth-century coffee houses near the university. I walked and walked every street inside the *Ringstrasse*, the street that encircled the old part of the city, loving the sense of getting to know this great city. My weeks were structured around attending classes five full mornings a week, learning beginning, intermediate, and then advanced German. I kept myself busy working, too. For two months that fall of 1963, I lived with an Austrian family I worked for as an *au pair*.

Every couple of weekends, I packed a small bag and took the train out to the *Schloss* to visit Fritz. On one of those visits, I sat in the forest-green den, drinking white wine with Fritz and his mother, Cousin Anna—they were used to his antics, I'm sure—when an announcement came over the wireless. "President Kennedy has been shot in Dallas." I reeled back in shock. "What?" The floor fell away, and I instantly felt homesick for my fellow Americans. My eyes went blank and fixated on the inkwell on the desk near me while my fingers clutched the velvet edging of the cushion I sat on. I kept thinking, *November 22. It's my sister's birthday, that's all I know about this day.* The passing of this bright light of a president shook my sense of security, leaving me topsy-turvy, dejected, and lonely. Nothing like this had ever happened during my short life. I felt disoriented and far away from familiar home.

A couple of weeks later, as Fritz and his mother and I sat around in the same dark-green den at the Schloss drinking wine, Cousin Anna held up an unopened letter from Cinch. "Read it to me," she said. "My eyes are tired."

I opened the envelope and read the letter aloud.

Dear Cousin Anna,

Thank you so much for the long and happy visit we had. I've always loved coming to visit with you. However, I want to apologize that we brought Marilee with us. I had no idea that she spent time in a mental hospital, or I never would have thought to bring her.

My fingers tightened on the edge of the weighty cream paper. What? *Bitch! What the hell is she saying?* My insides ignited, and the heat burned a circuit in my solar plexus. I looked up, insides still exploding, and dutifully continued reading.

We never should have brought her with us to see you. I apologize from the depths of my heart.

With love, Cinch.

Cousin Anna hooted out loud, the tip of the cigarette in its long silver holder dripping ashes as she gestured in the air. "What is Cinch thinking?" she said. "Don't listen to this. We welcome you here. Never pay attention to what others say about you. I know very well. I was raped by the Russians and had many people say unpleasant things to me. I learned very quickly, pay no attention."

I took comfort in her words and felt affirmed, but the fire in my belly remained. And an old familiar sheathing of shame engulfed me.

I returned to Vienna and then, *Frohe Weihnacten!* Merry Christmas! Back to Styria and singing "Silent Night" and "O Tannenbaum" with Fritz, Cousin Anna, and their family. As was the tradition on Christmas Eve, everyone showed up in regional costume, except Fritz's Belgian aunt, who wore a gorgeous Chanel suit. I reveled in wearing my new silk dirndl and fit right in. It felt festive and reminded me of the fun of Mardi Gras events. After cocktails, laughter, and much singing, someone rang a small hand bell signaling the time to admire the elegant, freshly cut, divine-smelling Christmas tree decorated with lovely old ornaments, tinsel, and real lighted candles.

We exchanged presents and sat down at the table decked with red-and-forest-green linens to eat a fabulous dinner of meat salad and roast goose, cucumber salad, apple puree, mushroom rice, more salad, and rich chocolate mousse—nothing but egg yolks, sugar, and chocolate topped with fresh whipped cream. As I ate, I listened to the tinkling of Fritz's aunt's rings against her glass half filled with red wine and the light clang of forks on china. The conversation ranged from stiff and formal to teasing, and alternated among German, French, and English. Fritz's young niece and nephew enlivened the night, but it was nothing like the party I knew my family would be celebrating in New Orleans—where no doubt friends trickled in, danced, drank, and talked until three in the morning. Observing the *Gemutlickeit* of this family gathering, I felt homesick for my own family.

I was thrilled when Fritz gave me a set of Augarten china—coffee and tea pots, sugar and creamer, cups and saucers with painted depictions of the heads of local animals prevalent in the Austrian wilds: goats, stags, deer, grouse. I was touched at his thoughtfulness, grateful to be spending time with his family at Christmas, and in spite of the incredible loneliness that I only acknowledged much later—the longing to be with him—I went on, head down, relishing any contact I had with him.

After New Year's, in the dead of Vienna's deepest cold, my au pair job at an end, I moved back into Fritz's unoccupied Viennese apartment, Am Heumarkt, across from the beautiful statue of Mozart playing a violin. The rent was free, that was a gift, but it was January, freezing, and every day I worried about whether I would be able to heat the space. The heating system presented a delicate challenge. Evenings I coaxed and serenaded the six-foot-tall baroque white ceramic stove. Fritz had instructed me how to start a fire, but I was no Girl Scout. When I eventually managed to light the stove each evening, the heat poured into the room. Warmth, for heaven's sake! Thawing, I would dive under the thick feather comforter and immerse myself in my German books. In that apartment, under the down comforter, I haltingly read *Siddhartha* by Hermann Hesse, and delighted in Friedrich Durrenmatt's Swiss mysteries, dictionary by my side.

I would fall asleep with my books as sweet companions—until it was time to get up in the frigid morning air to dress for class and head out to the university.

At the end of January, in Vienna one night, Fritz sat me down over dinner. "Since Maja and I are officially engaged now," he said, "and planning a wedding in May, I need to focus on that relationship."

Stricken, I asked, "What does that mean?"

"It means we cannot sleep together any longer, dear Marilee."

I imagined his fiancée had given him an ultimatum, because he would have no compunction about having a mistress. Not that I could see myself as such.

He leaned forward and squeezed my hand, his long eyebrows squinched together, forehead wrinkled, his smile rueful. "But I assure you I will still be your friend, and I will be here for you while you are in Austria."

My heart shrank. I could see him backing away, taking care of obligations in his different realms, getting ready for changes, keeping order in his life. He wasn't exactly cooler toward me— he was always warm in my presence, would touch my arm—but I detected a shift and grew sad that there might be no under-the-table flirting in restaurants, or running off to the guest room at the *Schloss*. I wanted to think he felt conflicted, but he was on a traditional aristocrat's path of keeping his promise to his betrothed. I was learning what it meant to play second fiddle. But I sat there quietly. I didn't want to alarm him with the extent of my feelings. He might run away, and I needed him, even if it wasn't as a lover.

My insides burned. I knew this wasn't a fairy tale, but I hadn't figured on having this depth of feeling for him. I felt as if I were losing my best friend, my best ever lover, and yet I certainly wasn't his best anything. I'd felt the same way when I had discovered I was my first lover's French Quarter chick and that all along he'd had a serious Newcomb girlfriend—later his wife—who was away on her junior year abroad in Paris. And when Daddy moved out of our household, drinking a lot and spending his time at movie theaters, I felt the same disconnect as now. I had settled for second best before, and it seemed to be a pattern. And it felt awful, living here in Austria, so far away from home. I'd left my roots behind and was looking for a new place to fit in, and this wasn't it. Still, I had to admit to myself that I loved the adventures I had experienced while getting involved with Fritz.

After Fritz's pronouncement, he continued coming to Vienna to take me out. He made certain I experienced the major social events of the city. I loved waltzing with him at Jaeger Ball dressed up in my silk dirndl, thankful I knew how to waltz. The joy of the music and the movement, one-two-three, one-two-three, carried me around the large, crowded, gilded ballroom as he nodded and winked to his elegant friends. After the ball, at the restaurant *Drei Husaren*, we flirted in a fraternal kind of way—with great humor—and drank a good Riesling, but I missed the fun and the teasing that drew my staid self into more playfulness, and, of course, I missed the physical closeness.

I knew the shift had to come, and I knew our deal had only been for that year. Adept at stuffing feelings, I convinced myself that as long as we were still friends I was okay. I knew he had feelings for his fiancée, maybe even loved her, but I judged that the real Fritz wasn't showing up with her. It never occurred to me to challenge him about what was happening. I didn't talk about it with him. Conflict would be too painful, and I was grieving enough as it was. The days of rolling in passion in the sheets decorated with red cardinals at the *Schloss* had disappeared, and there were no more afternoons squealing and laughing and rolling around on the cots in his hunting cabins.

Still, we didn't miss a beat in terms of getting together. One fine day we got into his red-and-black Porsche and drove northeast to Burgenland, where we ate a lovely lunch overlooking Hungary.

"Here, Marilee," he said, turning to me in a shop near the restaurant. "Pick out one of these dark-green jade boxes and buy it for yourself as a memento of being in this region of Austria." I bit my lip, selected a handsome box with sterling silver trim, and took out my wallet.

Another day in Vienna, we visited Demel's, and I shipped off to my family in New Orleans a box of the finest and tiniest Viennese chocolates packaged in red boxes shaped like miniature chests of drawers. We also spent hours poring over maps of every province in Austria, and he meticulously helped me plan bus trips to each one. We walked to a nearby elegant café and devoured delectable sandwiches. With his guidance, I built up a whole list of Viennese experiences, and, being me, I appreciated them, because I didn't understand that I deserved more. I ignored the soft voice inside that said, *You deserve someone for yourself.* Fritz taught me about a particular kind of rarified generosity—the ability to so elegantly choose for someone or to do something absolutely perfect for them. I had to give him that.

"You've got to go to Kitzbuhel and, of course, Salzburg," he said, "and then later to Greece and Istanbul." He encouraged me to keep on trekking to the reward of extraordinary views.

And so I allowed myself to continue in this brilliant love-affair-without-sex, and still felt embraced, swept away, passionate with abandon. That had not disappeared.

I stayed at the *Schloss* often that spring. One day, close to the wedding day, I walked with Fritz's friends to the local train stop to meet him on his arrival from a visit to his fiancée in Munich.

His friend Johan shouted, "I've got to tell him. This is wrong for him. He mustn't marry her. It won't work." He went on,

"Marilee, we all know he's much more comfortable with you. He is himself! He must not marry Maja, and today I'll tell him so."

"Oh, it's too late for all that," I said. And yet my heart pounded at the idea that maybe, just maybe, this wedding wouldn't take place. I allowed myself a few minutes to contemplate the idea that I should be the one marrying Fritz instead of the woman from Munich.

When his train stopped at the platform, Fritz bounded down the steps. "Hello, dear friends!" he said, "I am ready for this wedding to happen. Let us go have some dinner and I will tell you about my weekend."

What a year it had been, and yet I knew in my heart that I was not cut out to live in Fritz's country, or with him, even if my parents seemed titillated that Fritz was a baron, real royalty— not make-believe! I knew well that he was not in my future, but a girl can fantasize. And I had done that.

Three days later, my bag packed, we all drove to Munich for the wedding. My mother had shipped me one of my debut dresses to wear, long and silver blue. I pinned my hair up high and decided to have a good time. At the reception, I settled into meeting people, congratulating the bride and groom, smiling, drinking, and eating from the artful display of hors d'oeuvres. I danced with the man Fritz had introduced me to, but I did not dance with Fritz. Hats off to the bride. I fought looking at Fritz at every turn. And I drank a lot of champagne.

Before the wedding, Fritz, in his inimitable way, had arranged for me to meet his mother in Istanbul. "You can take the Orient Express down to Greece and travel there for two weeks, then get back on the train and go to Istanbul. Mother will come straight down from Vienna, and you can meet her and stay in rooms next to each other. Then Maja and I will arrive from our honeymoon tour in Iran, and we'll all have a couple of days together."

I grabbed at the chance—happy to be included in his life—and rode the Orient Express and traveled for two weeks around Greece with new friends I had met who were on the faculty at Princeton, and then I continued on to Istanbul.

At first, I swallowed the pain of being around the newlyweds. I had become adept at suppressing my feelings and focusing on the practical. Maja and I even shared a bathhouse at the beach, and, of course, I compared her tiny, well-shaped legs to my not-so-delicate larger ones. She behaved cordially toward me; however, I can only imagine now the feelings she suppressed being around this upstart American girl who siphoned attention away from her relationship with Fritz. She probably wasn't happy the morning Fritz and I took a boat trip on the Bosporus Straits and enjoyed a breakfast of fresh fish and fresh air with the Black Sea as a backdrop. It was a little heaven on earth for me to sit across the table from him one more time.

Whenever I felt dispirited, I rationalized my continuing loyalty by thinking about the times Fritz had been generous or full of fun or attentive toward me. It would take decades for me to see how I discounted myself. And wasn't it curious that Fritz's ego compelled him to make these kind gestures to me, spreading around his baronial self? Kindness of his heart? Or staccato displays of narcissism? Ironically, Fritz's tight-knit social group reminded me of the Uptown New Orleans crowd I was moving away from. Perhaps that is one reason I continued to fit myself into the fabric of his life—it reminded me of home, of belonging.

However, the benefits were many, not the least of which included awakening to a playfulness I had never known, a passion I had never felt. The incredible fun we experienced together eclipsed the loneliness of a string of nights spent by myself and by the acceptance of Maja's role. I felt high for much of those months with Fritz. If I had known anything about bipolar disorder at that time, I might have questioned the predominance of highs in my life that year.

As spring progressed, some part of me opened a window toward thoughts of home.

After a brief trip to Yugoslavia with Fritz, his new wife, and his family, I boarded the train for Ravenna and spent three days looking at the fabulous Byzantine mosaics there while I waited for my ship's departure. I had brought all my University of Vienna credentials, hoping to be accepted as a junior at Newcomb College in New Orleans. Another life. My return voyage took twenty-six days, providing plenty of time for reflection on my year abroad, and for some adventurous social time on board as well. I understood how I could never have thrived in Fritz's world. Titles of nobility, though outlawed in Austria in 1919, were still important to him and his family and, as baron by inheritance, Fritz would always live by the strict codes of his social class.

For several years after I returned, Fritz wrote me occasional letters on blue *par avion* paper. I loved his handwriting and tried to emulate it with the Pelikan pen he had given me. I even purchased and named a dog "Fritz" after returning to the States.

I didn't fully let Fritz go until thirty years later, when he came to New Orleans with a woman friend, having divorced Maja and two subsequent wives. He was still charming and flirtatious, though his jokes were tired. I blessed him on his way, glad to be married not to him but to my husband Ed. I had left the world of kings and queens and make-believe and fairy tales long ago by this time. I had come a long way.

Chapter 8

THE *f*ALL

O f all of the photographs taken when I was a young woman, which one did my mother choose to display in her well-appointed living room? Not shots of me laughing and being myself, having fun, or relaxing in my backyard under the banana tree. Not playing tennis or mothering my young children. And not one of my husband Tom Snedeker and me smiling. No, she chose the formal 1968 engagement photograph taken by a fancy social photographer in New York City. I guessed that this photo fit her notion of what her well-heeled oldest daughter should look like. Of course, at the time, I had worked hard to achieve exactly that effect.

Years later, I remembered the good-looking young woman in the photograph—her innocent smile and clear skin. What made me chuckle, though, was the volume of lustrous hair tumbling over her shoulders, thanks to the fall her mother insisted she wear, despite the sweltering summer heat, the fall she'd worn the entire winter since Tom and she started dating. If you were born after 1955, you might wonder, "What's a fall?"

In 1968, the year I married, it was a mandatory piece of equipment for fashionable young ladies. A fall was a false hair-piece that attached to your own hair, the same length as your hair but providing volume, with a comb sewn on to hold it firmly in place. You would slide it into the hair toward the back of your crown so that your own hair—in my case, already bountiful, a bit longer than shoulder length and rich brown—would look fuller and maybe even glamorous.

When I first saw it, I knew the photograph was a triumph. It embodied all that I felt I needed to reach for—all that was expected of me to be a successfully betrothed woman in the social class in which I was raised. In the portrait, my big gray-hazel eyes gaze eagerly into the camera. I wear a white wool sleeveless dress with a small standing collar. I can still feel the itch of the wool against my bare skin—but it looked right. It suited its purpose. My earlobes are adorned with fourteen-karat gold earrings, the only real gold ones I ever bought myself—eighty-five dollars on Madison Avenue in 1968. When I found them, I thought, "*Yes, these will do nicely*," and then forked out the equivalent of half a month's rent. The money I spent for the dress, earrings, and fall were well worth the price because of the fabulous portrait. This portrait, this engagement, this marriage-to-be to my tall, dark-haired, and handsome Cold Spring Harbor, New York, fiancé all affirmed my chosen path at that time.

In my photo, I see myself as a suitable fiancée for my future husband—the Uptown New Orleans girl working for *Antiques* magazine in New York City. As if the photo were not enough, the written newspaper announcement sealed the deal. My credentials—boarding school, attendance at Wellesley (even if I did stay only a year and ten days), the requisite list of Carnival balls from my debut year, attendance at Harvard and Boston University, graduation from Newcomb College in New Orleans, and brief study at New York University's Fine Arts Institute before I began work at *Antiques*. And Tom's pedigree was his prep school and college, his New York clubs, not to mention the fast-track post at First City Bank where he was then working. According to the way we were represented in the newspaper, we were set up for a lifetime of the right stuff.

At our wedding party on my grandmother's lawn in Biloxi, standing under the spreading, sheltering oak, dancing and drinking champagne and greeting 350 friends, I had a nagging worry. How would I possibly manage to remove the fall when Tom and I were in the same room? While Nain's New Orleans maid, in her crisp black uniform with white lace-trimmed apron and cap, handed me over to Crutcher, who escorted me down the freshly mowed grass aisle, it consumed me to the point that guests' faces on either side were a blur. I worried about it when I saw Tom and his best man standing next to the Episcopal priest under the beloved oak tree where we exchanged vows. I touched my veiled hair involuntarily more than once during the reception, and at the agreed-upon hour, when I went inside my grandmother's house to change into my red-and-blue trousseau going-away outfit, I checked on my hair again, making sure the bobby pins were holding firm. Then Tom and I said our good-byes to friends and family.

I thought, *we are leaving, and this party is just starting.* That's odd, how did we let that happen? It was as if the whole wedding experience were being truncated. I felt cheated, incomplete, which added to my apprehension about the next couple of hours. *And what about my fall?*

The thought of disclosing the existence of my fall to Tom mortified me. I loved him and had committed myself to our marriage, but we didn't know each other that well. Although we'd certainly shared some intense experiences such as hearing the news that his mother had suddenly died, which seemed to have bound us together, in looking back we had never built a platform or a genuine history for the deep sharing of our real needs and desires—in good part, certainly, because I didn't know my own needs and desires. These were uncharted waters. At the Mardi Gras mixer at Harvard when we had met, during my freshman year at Wellesley, we had spotted each other from across the crowded room. I couldn't look away as we snaked through the room to meet each other. I was definitely attracted to him and thought, *I could make babies with this man.*

We saw each other the next day, and while we were fumbling around on top of his uncle and aunt's bed in Newton (they were away), the phone rang. Tom had jumped up and answered it, and I watched the color drain from his face. It had gone something like this:

"Yeah, what time, Dad? Where? Who found her? How are my brothers?"

"No, Uncle Edwin is up in New Hampshire." He closed his hand over the mouthpiece and reported with a neutral expression, "My mother just died at home in Cold Spring Harbor."

I was stunned and speechless. So I cried for both of us.

Later that day, Tom said something like, "Every time my mom took the car out, I was afraid that she'd hit someone or drive into a ditch. She hasn't been right for a while."

When we went back to school for the spring term, he wrote letters to me from Hebron, and I wrote him back from Wellesley. In the fall, when he heard I was in McLean, he had come to visit me at the hospital, but my psychiatrist had sent him on his way back to Trinity College in Hartford, where he was a freshman, saying I couldn't have visitors for a while.

A year later, after I left McLean, took summer classes at Harvard, and after fall classes began at BU, Tom and I had two dates, the first sitting in freezing cold bleachers watching Harvard play football when it was too cold to talk. The second date, when I rode the train down to Hartford for a college weekend, about did me in; the travel on the train and being on the campus overrun with students and teachers was too much for me. I can still see the ivy-covered stone corridors stretching between buildings. Going into Tom's fraternity house was the last straw. Surrounded by people who seemed out of control and Tom, who readily joined the party, I begged off and grabbed a bus back to Boston and the quiet familiarity of my tiny Cambridge apartment. This was also during the same time I was flying back and forth to New Orleans for my debut. I was miserable and did not have the wherewithal to be the party girl in this setting.

Tom and I didn't see each other for the next four years. During that time, I was busy with my debut, hiking after the baron, and graduating from Newcomb in New Orleans. After I'd finished college, I enrolled in NYU's Institute of Fine Arts in September 1966. I stayed only one semester for lack of money—and that lack of groundedness that haunted me. Then I got an advertising job with *Antiques* magazine. I ran into Tom at a mutual friend's cocktail party in New York. We went to the movies a couple of times, just friends catching up—it felt great to see him again—and then in the fall of 1967, when I was a bridesmaid in our mutual friend's wedding in Hyannisport, my date failed to appear, and Tom's girlfriend chose that night to break up with him.

By Sunday night of that autumn Hyannisport weekend, we had gravitated to each other again. What a relief to be with someone familiar. I liked him. The next night, at dinner in Manhattan, I introduced him to Crutcher, who happened to be in New York on business. Crutcher didn't know it, but he gave the seal of approval when he said, "Tom's an attractive person. I'd hold on to him." He would say the same thing about Ed, twenty years later. Within a few months, Tom and I were engaged and planning a Biloxi wedding under the huge spreading oak tree where my parents had had their wedding reception, where my mother and her siblings and decades later my sisters and I had dug for Indian treasure, where we had played for hours in its shade.

In July of 1968, in our spacious honeymoon suite in the Biloxi Broadwater Hotel, facing the Gulf of Mexico, I slowly took off my shoes and stepped out of the two-piece, short-sleeved, silk getaway dress. I was killing time while Tom crashed around, searching for his suitcase, looking as awkward as I felt.

All I could think of was the fall. *Do I leave it on for the anticipated bridal sex scene? Would it come off in the bed?* I would be too embarrassed to take it off in front of him. Tom went into the bathroom. I found my white satin trousseau nightgown and slipped it over my head. So far, the hairpiece was still firmly in place. Tom emerged from the bathroom, threw his clothes over a chair, and dove onto the bed. He was talking fast about the reception, the people, the chartered sailboat where we would spend our honeymoon in Maine, and slurring slightly, paying little attention to me. Was he drunk? Or nervous? Remembering that the last couple of times we had slept together had been tense, my anxiety mounted. This was my new role, wife, and I wanted it to be perfect. If it meant wearing a costume, I would do that.

He lay back, looking relaxed, stretching his muscular hairy arms over his head, mumbling. I moved into the bathroom to brush my teeth. When I returned, Tom was snoring on the bed, a deeply regular rhythm already established. My first reaction was hurt. "How could he crash on our wedding night?" But soon I felt relieved. I returned to the bathroom to wash my face and remove the fall.

The next morning I almost pushed him out of our room to go find coffee for us before he visited the bathroom and discovered my luscious chestnut locks in the trash can. The housekeeper cleaning our room after we left must have been surprised to find the fake hair.

Tom never noticed that my hair didn't extend halfway down my back, thick as a horse's mane. Now it seems like a scene from a good comic film, but it's also a little breathtaking to realize how determined I was to be desirable and glamorous, how extreme the measures I took to be someone other than who I was.

Chapter 9

Season of
Discontent,
or Her-Story

In 1976, when I was pregnant with our third daughter, Tom and I decided we wanted more living space. We purchased an early-nineteenth-century, raised Louisiana cottage with high ceilings and a wide central hall, structurally sound but needing renovation. While it had once been a mayor's residence, then at the turn of the century a funeral home, and later the office of a proctologist, little trace of its history remained after we remodeled our quarters. With a down payment that used up trust money from my grandfather, and after spending two years and thousands of dollars on credit, we brought the orphaned dwelling back to life and stoked up some goodwill in our Garden District neighborhood.

Then we sat back and took a deep breath—our home was completed, we had a toddler daughter, Jennifer, and our older daughters, Anne Phyfe, six, and Rebecca, nine, were happily attending nearby Trinity School. Tom's work for a local engine distributor company seemed to satisfy his career needs for the moment. A Long Island New Yorker with his own club pedigrees now linked by marriage to my father, stepfather, and grandfather, and, being a likeable fellow, Tom joined several men's clubs and Carnival krewes.

I became earnestly active in the Junior League at age thirty, even though I shook in my boots whenever I led a committee meeting or spoke publicly. I always worried about what people were thinking. I didn't want to make a fool of myself. I was united with my mother in our dislike of public speaking—she could barely bring herself to read minutes at her Garden Study Club gatherings—and it took awhile for me to break through that ceiling. I wondered but never asked my sisters if they too had been similarly affected by Mom's reticence in a public setting. I attended meetings of both the Garden Study Club and the Junior League as a third-generation member. Life from the outside was good. Inside—being with myself—felt empty. I pushed aside my own needs and desires as I tried mightily to fit in with social expectations, having little idea that I could be making different choices. Numb with the effort, I suppressed sighs while plunging ahead.

Then one autumn day in 1978, two friends of mine arranged to visit from the West Coast. Unbeknownst to me, their stay sowed seeds of confusion in me. In 1965, before I married Tom, I had met Dick and Sharon Webster through a friend when they arrived in New Orleans to work on a yacht back in 1964. The next year I had visited them in San Francisco and then at Dick's parents' house in Mendocino overlooking the Pacific. While in California, I'd visited the campus at the University of California at Berkeley and fallen in love with the hills and the air and the sunshine and what seemed like a looser way of life than what

I knew in New Orleans. When I returned to New Orleans, I applied for and was waitlisted for a Woodrow Wilson Fellowship at Berkeley, but my parents scuttled the idea.

"It's too far away," my mother said. "Think of all the air tickets." They were sending my five siblings to private school with airfares, and Crutcher had always told me I was on my own after college. I think they also thought I wasn't ready for such a new environment after my stint in McLean. And I wasn't sure I was either. I didn't see myself as having the wherewithal to take such a step without their approval.

So I shifted direction, worked as a real estate agent over that summer of 1966, and made enough money to get myself to New York, where I began graduate school at NYU. Manhattan was in the backyard of New Orleans compared with California, as far as my parents were concerned at that time. With the money I'd saved from my one commission and by working part time for a writer and a professor, I was able to manage rent and tuition. At least for a while. I miscalculated how far my savings would go, and oops! After one semester, I quit and found a job. There was no question that I was naïve about money matters. So, early in 1967, I went to work as an advertising assistant for *Antiques* magazine, enjoying the thirty-block walk to my office building on 47th Street—from a tiny apartment located across from a spewing Con Edison smokestack through the concrete forest around me. At least I had escaped New Orleans.

Here it was more than a decade later, and the Websters were visiting New Orleans en route to Mexico and the Galápagos. Their way of life couldn't have been more different from mine and from Tom's—although he was open to their stay for my sake. They'd traveled across country in a baby-blue VW. Arriving at our house, they parked their van, dusty from crossing the desert, in our backyard, where they slept. While Tom worked twelve-hour days, in suit and tie, at the engine company,

I reveled in long discussions with my friends over iced coffee, beer, and wine, and enjoyed daytime forays into Parasol's in the Irish Channel, ten blocks away, for beer and oyster po-boys. We laughed a lot and retraced their trek across the country. I envied them their free and carefree existence. Spending time with the Websters was like finding water in the desert. For the first time, I questioned what the hell I was doing fulfilling so many others' expectations.

Maybe he was oblivious to the careless fun I was having, but when Tom was invited to come play with us, he said he was too busy working, and honestly, I didn't bat an eye. I wanted to continue feeling part of this welcome different way of life. I enjoyed the otherness of the visiting company. Sitting on the yellow sofas of our new house with sunlight streaming through the tall windows, Dick and Sharon asked me questions that I could hardly begin to answer. "How do you like living this way?" "Do you enjoy going to so many cocktail parties and Carnival balls and meetings?" "Do you ever get to let your hair down?"

Thus began my season of discontent. My local friends seemed satisfied with their lives, not that we talked about it. Only my therapist (one of a series) knew about my discontent—and not all of it. Who else would put up with my shit? But I couldn't see clearly and, unconsciously, I was self-destructing because I didn't know how to break out of the patterns and traditions without destroying myself. I had tried to escape at college, then with the baron, but I didn't know how to do this. I drank more alcohol. And feelings for Dick erupted overnight, which, impulsively, I told him about while we were driving together to pick up wine for dinner. I don't know if the attraction was one-sided or not, but Dick looked surprised when I blurted out this declaration. He and I later exchanged an awkward kiss in the shed under the raised house while retrieving—what, a hammer? That kiss was it, but it was enough to stoke my imagination. While

Dick and Sharon, their daughter, and my oldest daughter were away camping for the weekend, I spent the time imagining a shadow future with Dick, sensing possibility.

Five minutes after their VW van returned to our backyard at the end of the camping weekend, Sharon marched into the house, livid, hands on her hips, expressing her disbelief at the situation I had ignited. Dick had told her what I had said, and she had given him an ultimatum. She said they would be leaving as soon as Anne Phyfe retrieved her things from their van. The reality check painfully pierced my oblivion, or almost, as I just couldn't get Dick out of my head. Later I realized it wasn't Dick I wanted, but a real life for myself.

Later that month, during a tennis weekend in Florida with Tom and five other couples, I tried to call Dick, and Tom overheard me. It was his turn to read me the riot act, unprecedented in my memory. The tennis weekend was a flop for us, and our relationship shifted from one of unconscious trust to wariness and wondering—the first visible snag in the fabric of our marriage. We kept up our regular routines, but it was like a warning gong, and the sense of permanence and security was gone. If the girls intuited this strain, it was internalized, never articulated.

The Websters' visit and their perspective on living created a hole in my tightly woven life. The old yen to spend time in the West seeped in. I yearned for the directness and freedom I had experienced there in 1965.

In the years after Tom and I married in 1968, I didn't think of my dreams of going west, because I had no idea how not to do what I was doing as a wife and mother in Uptown New Orleans. Life would be simpler, easier, if I just kept on doing what was expected of me—hosting, Junior League volunteer placement, Garden Study Club meetings, chauffeuring the girls to Mrs. May's music classes, going to parties with Tom and the Tennis Club group. Not that I was miserable. A big crack had opened up, causing me to engage in some risky behavior. I didn't see myself as wretched, but I was unsettled, destabilized. Or maybe I simply wouldn't let myself see how discontented I was. I'd had a glimpse of real dissatisfaction and longing for something different, and that set up a conflict. I served as co-chair of the Mayor's Committee for the International Year of the Child and learned how to fulfill that role in meetings at City Hall and other community venues. I began a half-time grant job at Newcomb College that focused on working women where I engaged with people from all over the community, all colors and faiths, and that felt right. But I was still sailing along in response to others' needs.

Around that time, about 1981, I met blonde, focused, energetic Suzanne Lacy—also from California. She arrived in New Orleans early in January for the National Women's Art Caucus that would take place in February. Suzanne had come six weeks early to organize local preparations for the caucus that included street artist performances. The day that I saw her from across Bourbon Street acting on a street corner in the French Quarter, my heart expanded; the boldness and directness of her approach stunned me.

Her team began generating fervor among local women in the organization to prepare the way for their main event, a "River Meeting." They planned a potluck supper for five hundred women to take place in the United States Mint building at the Mississippi River end of Esplanade Avenue bordering the French Quarter. Dear friend and artist Mary Sue Roniger had passed my name on to the group because she was not able to participate. In reflecting on that time, I realize I was the token Uptown married white woman and had been captured by the concept of community potlucks. I joined the diverse group of women who worked with Suzanne and the other artists. I was in awe because so many of them comported themselves with authority, accomplishment, intention, and some with grace. We created a network of women's potluck suppers in private homes across the city—gatherings hosted by a dozen or so women from assorted backgrounds—to build a platform for the huge citywide event. In my more expansive and idealistic moments, I could see the anatomy of New Orleans brightening and strengthening through this work. I was thrilled to participate in what felt to me to be such a salutary event, and luckily, the timing dovetailed with my current part-time employment at Newcomb—although it was a stretch to juggle babysitters for the girls.

One of the initial pre-caucus potlucks took place in the renovated Garden District home Tom and I shared. I rented a large round table for twelve women, including Suzanne, gathered from around the city. Most of the women I was meeting for the first time. Suzanne introduced me to Laverne Dunn, who worked either for the city or the state, I can't remember now. Laverne was the first black person to come to supper at my house aside from women who worked for me as babysitters and housekeepers. I remember being anxious about hosting her—a little knot of uncertainty in my gut, as this was uncharted waters for me—but I quickly got over myself. She was smart and fun. I was curious. I wanted to live differently, and I was eager to be part of this project. Later, Laverne and I would fly together to the University of Houston, Clear Lake, for the grand opening of Judy Chicago's *The Dinner Party*, ultimate bold behavior for me, the new feminist.

Participation in the work of feminism in my city, called by some feminists the crotch of the South, bastion of white supremacy, seemed then of utmost importance to me. From this time forward I would view power differently. Around the same time, my Wellesley friend and dorm mate, Jean Kilbourne, blew me away when she came to New Orleans to lecture to McGehee Girls' School alumnae and parents on the effect of advertising on women. Seeing a slide depicting a bottle of Tabasco turned upside down dripping red hot juice into a slit-open baked potato woke me up with a bang.

Maybe there were some McGehee alumnae or Junior Leaguers in the audience of the River Meeting supper event, but generally speaking, the League at that time did not seem feminist. Even if they had feminist leanings, they came across as dressed-up ladies strategizing and being "nice" while they changed the community—this was still Mardi Gras krewe country.

That final culminating River Meeting potluck took place on a Thursday evening. I remember what I wore—a black-and-rust-colored French silk pleated skirt and blouse—conventional, elegant, and comfortable. My mother, my youngest sister Allison, and Ruth Nobles—captain of her Carnival organization, where she presented debs at the celebrations, and maid and cook to my mother—showed up. It was a huge potluck affair. Mom brought roasted and salted pecans, Allison brought a big salad, and Ruth, in a tailored navy-blue dress, carried a sizeable pot of red beans and rice in her arms. I enjoyed the surprise and approval from kith and kin. I never did talk with Mom about the feminist drive behind the event, but she was proud that I'd played a role in a community event, even if she might have been blind to the feminist aspect.

As a local member of the event-organizing group, my role was to stand up and welcome five hundred women of many skin colors from every corner of the city and the country. When I looked out at the sea of faces, I heard the exuberant sound of overlapping conversations. I liked being up on the stage—the excitement, the associations with out-of-town guests, seeing the hundreds of faces gathered together. This felt different from speaking in front of the Junior League—here I was not playing a role someone else had carved out for me but doing something that generated passion in me from the inside. A New York artist, Mary Beth Edelson, dressed in army fatigues—a radical display in a Southern town—announced the different program parts. She announced that sturdy five-by-five-inch cards would be passed out printed with the word HER-STORY. Guests were invited to write on the cards the stories of the women who had influenced them most, and the cards would be collected and brought to New York. I often wondered what happened to those amazing stories, not that I made the effort to find out. Seeing art made by women whose intention was to change the world for women clobbered me over the head, and I knew I had to find my way to participate further. I wanted to create a life for myself, live my own story, and make use of this opportunity.

After the River Meeting event, I gave Suzanne a ride back from the US Mint to her boarding house. She asked me in for a cup of coffee, but I was far gone myself, and I was becoming nervous about being away from home so long.

"I am whipped, aren't you?" she asked. She drew herself up as if remembering something. "But I do want to say a couple of things before I go in." She sat up, fully alert now.

"I've seen throughout these six weeks of working together what a great person you are, so many talents, and a smile to light up the world."

I tried to take that in.

"What is important to you? What are your beliefs?"

There was no way I could answer her because I could not articulate my beliefs. I felt dumb, mute, even a little desperate. And I was mortified. I was so tired, I felt like crying.

Suzanne then said, putting her hand on my arm, "Marilee, I think you are talented and passionate, but you are not grounded. You have so much to offer, and you need to get a grounding that will give you the foundation for doing unbelievable things with your life."

I winced. She had just told me I was deficient. I sank inside. I already knew it, but hearing it was awful. She wouldn't be my friend unless I would be grounded. Sadness welled up in me. I knew something of her beliefs, her creativity, and her determination from working with her these six weeks and observing how she was focused and intentional, so I valued what she was saying, even though it hurt.

"You're not centered, not connected to yourself and your feelings, and until you know how to do that, you'll be spinning your wheels."

I said to myself, defensively, *How does one ground oneself? Abracadabra!* But in my body, her words rang true.

I said goodbye to Suzanne, and we agreed to correspond about any new developments coming out of the River Meeting.

I managed to fall into bed without waking up Tom, and morning came much too quickly. After the children took off for Trinity School Friday morning, I realized that I was beside myself with worry, exhausted and scared. I called a trustworthy and sensible laywoman, Jerry Faulkner, who led one of my church groups. Jerry agreed to meet me in the boardroom of the church at ten that morning. Worrying the whole ride, I parked my car and entered the tall, nineteenth-century, salmon-colored Trinity Church where I was a congregant. I hurried past the receptionist, the church secretary's office, the priests' offices, and headed for the boardroom in the undercroft. Jerry was already seated and waiting for me. She stood and crossed the room to give me a hug, and then we sat on a sofa facing each other.

"Marilee, I'm so glad we can get together," Jerry said. "How can I help you this morning?"

I don't remember what came next, how much I told her about what was going on. Whatever it was, Jerry listened to every word. She listened to my body. She listened to my heart.

Her attention never faded. When I started weeping and wailing, Jerry kept on listening and pretty soon wrapped her arms around me.

After three hours together, Jerry and I stood up, and she placed her hands on my shoulders, saying, "Marilee, here's what I think might be helpful right now. I will call Tom at his office and ask him to pick you up here."

"But I have a car here . . ."

"Not a concern, he can pick it up later. I'm going to tell Tom you should take aspirin with some hot milk and go to bed for the weekend. He'll need to camp the children at someone else's house until Monday. And your job is to sleep all Saturday and Sunday. Your body and your mind need deep rest after being so busy for the past six weeks."

I was quiet and sighed. I knew I needed the rest, and I would never have taken that time for myself—I didn't know how.

"Someone else has to take care of the details now," she said, "for a few days anyway." I sighed again, with appreciation.

"Thank you. Thank you so much for being here for me."

In the weeks and months after that weekend, I knew on the deepest level that I was lovingly taken care of when I most needed it. This time, at least, attentive listening and rest worked. I was back on my feet, in the swing of things.

People pointed out various options to me, but I couldn't see them, so I chaired meetings, worked for the Junior League monthly rag, played more tennis, took the girls to Sunday school, and sat on Chippendale chairs at Garden Club gatherings. Tom supported my flurry of civic activities. I brought the girls to his Carnival parades and helped them climb tall standing ladders with makeshift wooden seats, where the girls caught beads thrown by maskers on the floats. I dressed up for cocktail parties, dinners, and Carnival balls, and picked out the palest sepia-color paint for the Washington Avenue hallway walls.

I spent more and more time at church services and meetings and was relieved to have this spiritual outlet for my energy. I liked learning more about the faith I had loosely grown up in. I studied Scripture out of curiosity. I also continued carpooling to schools and games, making sandwiches, stripping the string off celery, and drawing pictures on lunch bags—but the tension inside me only grew.

I believed I was on a spiritual path and, during 1980, I sought mentoring to explore becoming a priest. A pivotal moment in my search to be grounded had been reading a long article about the initial group of women ordained into the Episcopal priesthood. That did it for me. I got it in my head to follow their lead.

A week before the 1981 Mardi Gras, Tom and I attended a three-day intensive Episcopalian retreat on Christianity. He'd come along at the recommendation of the priest who suggested I attend this Cursillo as a first step in exploring priesthood. I felt anxious about Tom accompanying me, self-conscious and maybe stifled by him being privy to this previously private part of my life that I was awakening to. Part of him respected my new intention. I think he was trying to be open to it and supportive, but he must have been wondering about the whole idea.

On the Monday after the exhausting three-day Cursillo, following three sleepless nights lying on a narrow, lumpy cot, while Tom slept fitfully in the men's dorm, I kept my appointment with the rector to keep him apprised of my pursuit of priesthood and my progress.

As I look back, I realize I had little understanding—and not enough sleep on that occasion—for what I was exploring. I told the rector that I wanted to celebrate the sacrament, the Eucharist, to help people understand and care for themselves and others, to bring the presence of a woman priest to congregations, and to attend to elderly and hospice patients. I told him I had taken steps to meet with other women priests in Houston and New York and felt this was my calling. The rector encouraged me and, at the same time, pointed out some of the realities of juggling a family and attending seminary away from home. I was concerned about how my studying for the priesthood could affect our family, but I remember dismissing the details from my mind, skipping over them.

I didn't tell the rector that one of the primary kickers most vivid in my mind that turned me toward pursuing priesthood had been attending the Good Friday services the previous Easter. The sight of five male priests stripped to their black cassocks, removing the sacred objects from the altar, with not one female priest among them, had nauseated me. This incident fueled my desire. I was on a crusade—first, to help see that my church would take on a woman priest and, second, to work toward becoming a priest myself. My fervor was a little over the top, but I couldn't see that. And I became more distractible and unstoppable. Something was changing in me.

Chapter 10

QUEEN OF
THE NIGHT

The River Meeting happened in February 1981. By the
time that year's Mardi Gras season was in full tilt, I was
exhausted once again, but I didn't say no to any of the parties
and balls. For six straight whirlwind days, starting with attending Ruth Nobles's black Original Twenties Ball that lasted until
the wee hours, Tom and I went from party to party to ball.
Going to Ruth's ball opened my eyes to a new world. Tom and
I sat in reserved, center-stage box seats, two of only five white
people in the ballroom, including the *Times-Picayune* society
editor Nell Nolan. After all the guests had been greeted by the
club president, Ruth appeared in a long white dress, long white
gloves, and a plumed white headpiece. With great dignity she
introduced and guided each of twenty young debs across the
floor, while the deb's name and family history were read out
loud. Men wore black attire, tux or tails—and were not masked.
Much applause and attention were granted to each young woman

walking across the floor as Ruth held up her left hand. This was an organized and dignified affair, and when Tom tapped me on the shoulder at two in the morning and said he simply had to go home so he could get to work at the bank the next morning, I was mortified. We were the first to leave, and I was anxious about our rudeness.

On the seventh of my whirlwind days, when I was already far too wound up from going nonstop, Tom and I attended one of his balls, the Krewe of Atlanteans, the organization Penny had been queen of during her debutante year.

My gown for Atlanteans had been ready and pressed since the start of the season in early January. For so long I had felt content to attend the balls. I had always thrilled at the sound of the "Triumphal March" from *Aida*, played when the king and queen first entered the ballroom; however, more recently, as the festivities started, the muscles in my legs would bounce restlessly, and my eyes would wander. I felt as if I were jumping out of my skin. Now when I attended a ball, especially since the experience of the Women's Art Caucus River Meeting, I felt trapped sitting with dozens of other women while we waited passively to be called out to dance at the beck and call of the maskers. Before that, I had loved the rush of the evenings when I was called out several times in a row, flush with the thrill of existing near the center of the activity on the ballroom floor, the performance of it. "Mrs. Snedeker is called out to dance." I would step over the satin-shoed feet of women perched on unforgiving wooden auditorium seats and make my way to the aisle to take the white-gloved hand of a committeeman dressed in white tails. He would lead me across the white canvas-covered dance floor near the king and queen's dais and hand me over to a masked dancer. I would feign surprise as I guessed at the masker's identity, took hold of his cotton-gloved hand, and thanked the call-out man. Sometimes I struggled to understand the masker's slurring and hiccupping. *Grin and bear it*, I told myself. It was all part of the game. Not that the men had a monopoly on the drinking. Women, including myself, brought purses big enough for slender silver flasks and rendezvoused in the ladies' room. After the dance, a committeeman would return me to my seat of privilege in the call-out section, where I would watch other people and wish for another dance—or at least for another drink.

But that year, midway through the Atlanteans Ball, seated in the call-out section, I began hallucinating. I became Queen of the Night. I remember being very sensitive to the way the medieval-style, tapered chiffon sleeves of my black dress felt on my skin. I remember stretching my arms out wide as a goddess—or priestess—invoking power. And I remember that I honestly thought I was queen of the ball. As far as I knew, no one noticed that I was slightly off. In some wee corner of my mind, I registered that I wasn't right, but my body went on autopilot as my mind wove a story in which I was the only star. At the Queen's Supper after the ball—a cocktail party held at the queen's house with African-American waiters passing drinks—I slurped down glasses of scotch and water while continuing to be my social self, an exuberant guest, the Queen of the Night surveying her subjects.

At one a.m. Tom, unaware that anything was awry, found me, put his mouth to my ear, and said, "Marilee, it's time to go. I have to show up for work in the morning." I demurred, too tipsy to care that I wasn't going home with him, and said I'd get a ride with my brother Bruce. With a determined expression on his face and a night of drinks under his belly (though I could barely tell he'd been drinking), Tom headed out. I went over to Bruce and tugged on his sleeve to ask if I could get a ride with him and his date. Twenty-seven years old at the time, he seemed to get a kick out of my inebriated state.

Hours later, in the car, I was giddy with the hilarity of our excursion, and for the entire drive downtown, Bruce and his friend laughed at seeing me acting so wildly. We parked on Madison Street, a block away from Jackson Square and Café du Monde in the French Quarter, walked a block, and sat at one of the small round marble tables. We indulged in the traditional *beignets* and *café au lait*.

My breath scatters white powdered sugar from the tops of the beignets, and I watch it cascade down my black chiffon ball dress. I laugh a mite too loud at my brother's joke and excuse myself, pushing away from the small round café table where he and his lady friend are still laughing, passing two confabbing waiters standing in front of the beignet cooker, zigzagging my way to the women's restroom. Alone inside the clean but shabby space, I peer into the mirror and grin. All's right with the world! I throw up my arms goddess style, my neck arched, and issue a belly laugh to all surfaces present, sending out blessings to the city. I open a stall door, lift my floor-length powdered-sugar-flecked ball dress high enough to clear the toilet, turn around, and sit down. Bless this city, pee and flush. May you be full of light, pee and flush. Bless the people who live here, pee and flush. May our city shine and all people live in harmony. Let the good times roll. With each flushing I beam messages throughout the entire citywide sewer system. What better way to pass on and distribute the light that I know I am to pass on? After what seems like sufficient blessing of the city, I stand up, smooth down the skirt of my gown, and peer satisfyingly at myself once more in the mirror. Then somehow I'm outside the restroom.

When I emerged from the bathroom, the two waiters gave me bemused looks. This wasn't the first time they had seen the glazed looks of drunken customers coming for *café au lait* and *beignets*. I tottered back to the table, and after a few minutes I took hold of Bruce's arm, and the three of us walked back to my brother's car. The car rumbled down streets and suddenly, with the sun on its way up, Bruce dropped me at home and I had to focus on mounting the seventeen steps to the front door of our house on Washington Avenue. I fumbled for my key, waved to Bruce and his friend, went inside, and slowly walked to the back of our wide hallway. I fell to my knees and placed my hands in prayer position. Tom came out of our bedroom white-faced, his voice tense. "My God, where have you been? It's six in the morning." Maybe he also said, "Are you okay?" I don't remember if I answered him out loud. I remained kneeling. And silent.

Then the girls, now awake on the floor above us, bounced down the stairs. Almost-eleven-year-old Anne Phyfe was first and came by way of the kitchen, where she poured herself some Cheerios before sitting at the dining table near me. She asked, "What are you doing there, Mommy? Why do you still have on your ball dress?" She pushed away from the table and came over to me. "Get up, Mom. Mom, why aren't you getting up?"

Rebecca looked on for a minute and disappeared to the space under the stairs in a niche behind my big loom. Jennifer was right behind her and cried for four or five minutes at the commotion, yanked on my unresponsive arm insistently, and then comforted herself with her doll. Before he left to drive the girls to school, Tom helped me up and guided me to my side of our big bed. He instructed me to call him at work if I needed him.

I had snapped, broken, gone manic and psychotic, but didn't know it, and I don't think that Tom knew it or wanted to recognize it. He must have had an inkling, maybe unconsciously, because he was familiar with my history, though we had never discussed it. Once everyone went off to school and work, I moved to the living room, sat on the sofa, called the church, and spoke with a young red-haired priest. I told him that I had received messages through my television screen to call someone there.

The red-haired priest promptly drove the six blocks over to the house and tried to talk with me to figure out what was going on. Finally, he said, resignedly, "You're broadcasting your thoughts. I think we need to call someone else in." Just as he said that, my dear friend Betsy Nalty telephoned me, and when I answered in a voice that didn't sound like my usual self, without further ado she drove to my house and relieved the priest. She was familiar with my history at McLean and alert to anything that might be off kilter. She took charge, turned down the covers on my bed, fed me consommé and tuna fish sandwiches, and hugged me and stayed with me—without judgment—while I lay catatonic in bed. She called Tom to come home from work and suggested that he find someone to watch the girls.

That evening, the Wednesday before Mardi Gras, I sat numb and silent in the front seat of our royal-blue station wagon as Tom and my sister Pixie drove me through the streets of downtown New Orleans. Tom steered the car in and out of the Krewe of Babylon parade floats and flambeaux carriers as we made our way to the Tulane Medical Center. He had called a friend to watch the girls that night. We inadvertently became part of the parade before driving into the parking lot of the hospital, the sounds of a rousing marching band reverberating in our ears.

After I was admitted, Pixie and Tom stiffly said their good-byes and left. I could hear their conversation as they walked down the hall.

"I'm calling Marilee's friend to come take care of the girls over the weekend," Tom said. "Jesus, it's parade time and Mardi Gras, and I'm riding floats on Thursday night and Monday night, and the girls will want to catch beads from me . . ."

"Give yourself time," Pixie said. "It'll all work out. Thank God Marilee came here without a fuss."

And there I was in the hospital once again, unable to take care of myself, much less anyone else, and conflicted as ever about the forces tugging at my fragile self that pulled me toward family and those who wrenched me toward my poorly grounded self. Everything seemed intensified.

Tom brought the girls to see me on the psychiatric floor one school night. I still felt as if I were in a bubble and wasn't talking much. I had a hard time relating to them so soon after being admitted. The medication—lithium—had not yet kicked in, and I was still in a low place. I had no idea what the doctors or Tom were saying about my break or whether he had shared this with his friends. Rebecca bounced on the bed, Jennifer hid in a cupboard and then sat on my lap, and Anne Phyfe asked me more questions: "Why are you here? How long will you be here? What do you do here? Don't you miss us?" Tom and I had little chance for an exchange.

After a three-week stay in the hospital—eight months and a week shorter than my McLean stay twenty years earlier—sleeping, attending therapy groups, and three weeks of medication (lithium) for a bipolar diagnosis, all the while carving daffodils on woodblocks and writing in a journal—I returned home to a house that seemed especially empty once my family left in the morning.

Back home, I resumed the routine of carpools, sandwich-making for the girls, and church meetings, trying not to wonder who knew about my recent experiences. I felt a little fragile around these carpool and churchwomen, uneasily standing around talking about tennis and Junior League and church meetings. It was hard to meet their eyes. I could feel them trying to keep things normal. My doctor at Tulane was gentle with me and helped me refocus on the things I needed—less stress, more sleep, no alcohol, lithium. My lithium seemed to be doing the job of bringing me into balance, preventing me from swinging up to those ecstatic highs of feeling so powerful and down to those drained lows of feeling fake, as if sheltered by a mask with no face underneath. But who was I? Queen of the Night? Wife? Mother? Crazy woman? Feminist? I was looking for my role, really for myself. I just had to catch up with this recast of myself as a person just off a psychiatric unit.

Later, in 1994, fifteen years after Barbara Gordon published *I'm Dancing as Fast as I Can*, I would read that famous memoir about her Herculean effort to overcome Valium addiction. I was overcome with recognition of her plight and her cold-turkey withdrawal from pills quickly followed by physical, mental, and emotional deterioration. I felt as if I were reading my story, and I swore at that time to write my own story one day. Both Gordon and Dr. Trautman were lifelines to me—Gordon in understanding the impact of nine years of taking amphetamines to lose weight, and Dr. Trautman, whom I saw when I was seventeen, in helping me understand my family dynamics. I understood how lucky I had been that lithium worked on first go-round and that I did not have to live through the horrible experiences Gordon had experienced with misdiagnoses and random medicinal cocktails. But I did still have a lot of confusion and work ahead of me figuring out who I was, what my ties to my family and tradition were, and what life I wanted for myself. The lithium was bringing me into balance, but it worked slowly, and for six years afterward I wavered, bouncing back and forth between highs of oblivion and lows of dullness.

Chapter 44

Two Priests

One day, about two months after my stay in the psychiatric unit at Tulane Medical Center, my mentor for the priesthood, the Reverend Dale, married with two children, rang my doorbell and announced that he was paying a pastoral visit to me at my home. I had attended one-on-one sessions with him in his office at his church to explore spiritual issues and talk theology; I believed he understood my intentions and questions regarding the human spirit—truly understood my soul-seeking. He would look at me with what seemed like deep understanding. And I felt a connection. In addition, he seemed to get feminism. Was I just seeing what I wanted to see? He was one of the five priests at my Episcopal church attached to the school where my daughters were enrolled. When he came to the house, Dale wore his stiff white collar, a light-blue shirt, black trousers, khaki jacket, and appeared earnest as he said, in his Southern accent, "I just want to make certain that all is well, that you've settled in here. Also," he added, "putting on my mentor hat, I'd be *happy* to talk over a few things that might be helpful on your path to becoming a priest." I ushered him into the double parlor and gestured for him to sit on the other end of the sofa from me, noticing and suppressing the odd feeling of being alone with him in my home, and not knowing quite what to do about it. We talked first about life after hospitalization, then about the ministry that we had just started co-leading, and finally the Old and New Testaments study group coming up.

"And when you're ready," he said, "I am eager to have you help me take the Eucharist to the ladies in the home." He reached over and patted me on the shoulder, his hand lingering there. He looked at me meaningfully and leaned closer. My body jumped to high alert. I was surprised, stunned—and fascinated. The touch felt good, this brief connection so inviting. I looked at him, curious, noticing not for the first time the odd, slightly uneven orange-peel quality of the skin of his cheeks; then we stopped talking, kissed, and groped some. I felt alarmed yet yielding—I couldn't pull away. Murky, murky waters.

After a couple of minutes, I did pull back and stood up to pull myself in, thinking, *This is my house. This is where my family lives. Stop!* But I was flattered by his attention, drawn to his intellect, and taken in by his second-class charisma. He seemed to understand me well. Reason simply evaporated.

I was seeing a therapist for prescribed meds, but I found it easier to turn to Dale to talk to. I had trouble sharing my deepest feelings. I didn't know what they were—it hadn't been so long since Suzanne Lacy had called me ungrounded—and couldn't discern them clearly. I decided that I'd better talk with a real person instead of endlessly pouring out my soul onto a journal page.

Was I still taking my medication, you might ask? I'm not sure of the exact timing, but I remember that for the first five years of taking lithium after my Tulane Medical Center stay, I went off and on the lithium several times while my psychiatrist and I experimented with dosages to find out exactly what would keep me from flipping into mania. So, with my lack of regularity, I was on and then off lithium, and at times I lost good judgment and acted out in ways I later regretted. To complicate matters further, I sometimes drank, which wiped out the benefits of the medication. I found myself drinking more alcohol, especially during the ensuing affair, even though I knew it was contraindicated with the lithium. Meds or not, I was hooked on this guy, and we scheduled meetings in odd places—mostly parking in his car at the end of Louisiana Avenue Parkway between Tchoupitoulas and Magazine streets near the river warehouses. I would look in both directions, get out of my car, and slink into his. We drank wine out of plastic glasses backlit by the street lamps. We would run into each other "accidentally" in the church undercroft, drive together to bring the Eucharist to the Home for Women, and schedule extra meetings for our joint ministries.

A year or so into my shrouded relationship with Dale, I turned forty—July 1982. My hardworking and unsuspecting husband, Tom, surprised me with a birthday party in our home that included good food and lots to drink, forty of our closest friends, among whom one was his future wife—vivacious with slender legs and blonde hair—and her current husband. The event was a success, but underneath my seasoned party face—the mask I had learned to wear so early and so well—and the excitement and tension of the affair, I began to lift my eyebrows and open my eyes. I began to rebel against the role I had been playing for almost all my life and had tried more and more frantically to perform perfectly during the last fifteen years of my marriage to Tom.

As the affair progressed, so did my thoughtless and reckless behavior. Months into the affair, at Sunday services, I sat just close enough to the church sanctuary and far enough away from

Dale's wife to exchange eyefuls of meaningful messages with him. Good God, someone must have wondered. I drank wine from his chalice two days after drinking wine in his bedroom. Hell, we drank glasses of wine in his blue-and-white bedroom in the middle of the day.

Foremost in my mind was my fear of running into the other older church woman he was seeing. He talked about her now and then and showed me where they met, in a small house one block down from Audubon Park, shades of flipping into a mood of little respect for myself as I had with the baron. Another time, I hid under a quilt in Dale's car so we could enter his garage without being seen as we drove by neighboring parishioners. One day, Dale appeared at a ministry meeting wearing a cream-and-maroon polyester zipper shirt, piercing my delusion of his perfection. This would not do. Maroon polyester did not fit into the aesthetics of my world. He was not a king, not a baron, not a fairy-tale man—in spite of his God-like authority as a priest and spiritual mentor. Not long afterward I presented him with a gift of a new black-watch plaid flannel shirt, and presto! He wore it occasionally and my pain disappeared. He fit my perfect picture for a little longer.

One night, we each parked our cars in front of a row of houses a few blocks from church, and when I got out of my car to get into his, a couple was descending the steps of their townhouse—oh, God, it was a church vestryman and his wife! I immediately put blinders on my blinders, stood still, and wiped the thought from my mind that they recognized me. I simply blocked them out. I was getting good at that. Actually, I think it was one of my major ways of getting through life, so it was nothing new. And I continued on to Dale's car as if everything were normal. I couldn't deal with the idea that someone might recognize me in this clandestine behavior.

Thank God for journals. I wrote and wrote in mine to help

sort out the conflict I felt. I was still trying to hook up with men in authority, kings, even as I rebelled. I think I wanted to be part of the elite powerful world and yet was rebelling against it because I wanted and needed to be myself, to be whole, to be well. But sometime in the middle of our affair, Dale prompted me to get rid of my journals "because someone might find them." Obediently, I wrapped up seven years of black-and-white composition notebooks in twine and sat on the top step of the front porch one morning, waiting for the sanitation truck to take them away. When I heard the grinding and gear-shifting of the truck coming down Washington Avenue as it bumped across the St. Charles Avenue streetcar tracks, I descended the remaining fourteen steps of the raised cottage with my precious bundle. The driver stopped in front of the house, and I ran into the street, took a jerky breath, and heaved the package into the sour, metallic-smelling jaws of the truck. I felt free for a minute, then lurched away, grief flooding every pore as it hit me what I had done, throwing away my heart, just because Dale had asked me to.

The girls had no warning about my unconscious momentum to break up my marriage—Tom and I rarely argued, never fought. We were so eager to be good parents and contributing members of our community that we didn't give our relationship the attention it needed. I didn't realize at that time just how important community service was for me. I needed a context in which I could feel competent and effective, and since I wasn't employed, the settings came through the Junior League. And I couldn't see how much intimacy we were missing because of my other goals. By that time, Dale was no longer on the church staff, and his wife had left town earlier in the summer. I sat down with Tom in July 1983, told him of my decision to separate, and bore his disgusted and white-faced reaction. Later that summer, I called all three daughters to the sofa in the living room—the same one where Dale and I had first touched. Tom, a good father, stood nearby, showing little expression. With almost no buildup, I said, "Your dad and I will not be living in the same home anymore."

My body jerked involuntarily when I heard the shrieks and tears that followed—at ages thirteen, ten, and seven, they had picked up no clues.

Anne Phyfe and Rebecca jumped up from the sofa, and each turned on me in disbelief. Jennifer crawled into my lap and cried at all the confusion. I told them I planned someday to be with Dale—and they howled. He was Father Dale to them, priest in their church and school; they were mortified. Hindsight, painful hindsight—that poor judgment, blunt and intrusive self-centered behavior that kept tripping me up. I can only describe myself as cold and detached at that time, and still nowhere near grounded. I wasn't grounded because I hadn't solved that tension for myself, for my wellness. I would never be grounded until I could deal with the conflict of wanting to belong and be recognized, valued in my family tradition yet needing to be myself. I was caught up in my misguided but immediate goal of going off with Dale.

Later, when I reflected on my relationship with Tom, I realized I'd often felt stifled by what I perceived as his need to control, though I know now it was partly the stifling I perpetrated on myself that I was feeling. His big, extroverted energy unwittingly swamped me in my ungroundedness and my own need to live up to others' expectations without examining my needs, my inner needs. I was trying to live someone else's life, not my own, and I couldn't be myself and grounded in that world until I shifted from living from the outside in to living from the inside out, and this had created a time bomb for our marriage. Did we ever break through to real intimacy? We had our moments, but I was so busy protecting myself from God knows what. And Tom with his work, his tennis, his krewes—he was busy too. I knew things weren't working. It wasn't just that we were both so busy. We were each playing the roles handed to us, Tom as well as me. That's what broke down the marriage—my being caught in a role that I tried to perform but rebelled against, a role in which I couldn't be present and be myself. I had to cast off the mask, just as I had cast off the fake hairpiece years ago on our honeymoon night. It was scary work, but I had begun.

That September of 1983, Dale, wearing a short-sleeved yellow guayabera, drove out of New Orleans in a rented truck. He had just been suspended from the priesthood by his bishop and directed to enter a rehab center. No one had mentioned the affairs he'd had with his parishioners. By this time, I knew he kept a bottle of wine in a drawer in his office desk. "You never know when you'll need it in this business." On the day he left town, we met two blocks toward the river from the church. He seemed maudlin and self-pitying. I spotted two gallon-size jugs of red wine sticking out from underneath a couple of towels on the floor on the passenger side of his car.

"Dale, what the hell are you doing with bottles of wine in the front seat of your car? How could you!" I had taken huge, if mindless, steps to spend my life with Dale—left my husband and frightened my children, stunned my family—but not to squander my life with someone who drank his way down the highway while driving to a rehabilitation center. It stung to think that he was such a fucking mess and in such a muddle—and that I was part of that muddle! Even so, struggling mess that I was, my loyal streak kicked in, and I stayed in touch with him over the next few months. I later realized that without the wine, he probably would not have made it to rehab without going into withdrawal.

After his treatment that fall, his brief suspension from the priesthood behind him, Dale was assigned to a church in a southern Louisiana town. One weekend while the girls were taking their turn with Tom, without saying anything to any of them, I drove seventy miles to visit Dale in his rented motor home with a plastic tablecloth and imitation wood paneling, such a contrast from the spacious, elegant, and beautiful raised cottage I had lived in with Tom and the girls. As I hung up my jacket in his closet, I spotted a cardboard box of men's magazines. I heard alarm bells go off, but my faithful blinders went up once again, and I stayed with him that afternoon, visited his little church, and spent too much time in his quarters. Dale subsequently moved to another parish in a different state. That spring—it's unbelievable to me now—I flew to see him and to check out his new city with the thought of bringing my daughters there to live.

During that trip, while I was driving around the town looking at houses with FOR SALE signs, a switch went off in my brain and heart, pockets of light broke through my clouded thinking, my perspective took a 180-degree turn, and I finally understood that life with Dale was not for me. A little more royal, please, less tacky circumstances. Had my attraction to him been a way to get out of my straitjacket of a role as a New Orleans high society wife without knowing that was what I was doing? I needed to get out, but not to Dale's world. I can't remember now if I told him face to face or simply packed up and flew back to New Orleans. I arrived home free from the notion of ever going off with Dale. Two months later I heard that he had married an older, well-established social worker in that city. I learned that during our affair, Dale had also been seeing the mother of one of my daughter's classmates who participated every week in our study group. He was working three of us! Again, shades of being one of the Baron's bevy when I was twenty-one and full of fantasies. Would I ever learn to value and stand up for myself?

The Easter after I walked away from Dale, I walked into a service at my church wearing a white, wide-brimmed, plumed hat in a crazy effort to hold my head up after the breakup. When I sat down by myself in a pew in the back of the church—the girls were probably at Tom's—I felt so self-conscious I could have vomited, but I carried myself tall, super tall considering the plumes, and supremely self-conscious, because it seemed too late to back down from my decision. My mood switched that quickly. When I had tried on the hat at home, I had been ebullient and thought it expressed exactly how I felt. I should have held back, but that was not my way. Act on impulse, dwell in remorse, and regret later was more like it.

Some months later, in Fall 1984, Father Thom Blair, the interim rector at Trinity, called me into his office. I assumed he had on his list of duties to make a pastoral follow-up with me since I'd had an affair with a priest of this church, or maybe he just wanted to check on me to see how I was doing after my breakup with Tom. We had briefly met, his sermons were traditional but sensitive, and I expected that he would be asking how he could help.

"How are things going for you since your separation?" he asked.

"I'm doing fine, Father," I said, smiling. You know, best foot forward. "My girls are fine." I looked up and knew something was awry by the disgusted look on his face. My shoulders screwed up tight toward my ears, and my neck shortened.

He asked a few more questions and then said, "You are not remorseful at all. It seems you have not reflected for one minute about the trouble that you are in and the pain you have caused." A mixture of regret and anger flashed across his face. "You're talking to me as if nothing has happened. I can't understand it."

I was stunned.

He shook his head resignedly, stood up, and gestured toward the door. "I can't help you. Goodbye."

His refusal to absolve me jolted me. I had secretly expected he would pat me on the shoulder and say everything would be all right. I felt deflated.

The consequence of his rebuff—a gift, certainly, but a painful one—resulted in my blinders beginning to drop away, and when I could acknowledge some of my issues, thanks to the priest's mirror, I eventually sought out counseling. I received kind and insightful help to face the feelings that came up, and guidance in integrating the realizations that were flooding in. At the same time, I began to accept that the priesthood might not be the right fit for me—I would never make it in so regimented an institution as the church. I had little interest in surrendering my needs and wants to such a life and grew grateful for the discernment. I flashed on the thought that social work might be a way to satisfy my interests. Just not yet.

Years later, I comprehended that every step of the way had brought me closer to knowing myself. My bipolarity and impulsivity have been something of a gift. If I weren't bipolar, I might not have needed so desperately to make the effort to dismantle old beliefs and patterns in order to embrace a full life. However, I recognized that the central tension in my life had been the tension of belonging and rebelling. That and the bipolar tensions and swings fed each other in a bad way.

Chapter 12

GOODBYE TO ALCOHOL, JUNIOR LEAGUE, AND NOBLESSE OBLIGE

During this time, and for the next couple of years, I was still testing out lithium under a doctor's supervision. At the same time, I kept drinking—one drink, two, more—negating the effects of the lithium, and eventually my balance and my judgment would go awry. On Christmas Day in 1986, I sat at Mother and Crutcher's big round dining table drinking the ritual glass of Dom Perignon with parents and siblings. It was eleven months after my divorce became official, and two years since the end of my affair. My off-kilter judgment burst forth in a manic frenzy: I gave my sister Pixie a book of lesbian poetry—no doubt a manifestation of my own curiosity in that realm; I gave my mother a vibrator; and I gave my stepfather a pair of red satin shorts. Pixie's face read dumbfounded first and then ticked off. Mom's face tightened up, repulsed. His face neutral,

Crutcher thanked me and tucked his gift back in its box. My brother Bruce said, "Well, I hope this isn't the start of something new." I had thought the gifts were so perfect at the time and hadn't a clue about their inappropriateness until everyone opened them.

Bruce was right, my lack of judgment that Christmas Day was the start of something new—a new awareness that led me to recognize and take the courage to leave my family and traditions behind, and to explore beyond the limits of the New Orleans world, to be myself without apology.

One Saturday in early spring of 1987, I found myself screaming at the girls—not for the first time.

"Clean up this table!"

"Mom!" This from Anne Phyfe.

"Get your things out of the breakfast room!"

"Stop yelling at us," Rebecca shouted.

"Stop crying!"

"I can't help it," Jennifer sniffled.

"Pick up your books!"

"No, Anne Phyfe, you can't go out with your friends today."

"Clean up the kitchen *now*, Rebecca."

I was horrified at my own yelling, how my face squinched up in fury. I wanted to stop but didn't. Finally, their reactions—surprise and shock and hurt, rebellion, and worse, resignation written all over their faces—got through to me. I heard myself—my irritable, aggravating, grating self—and grasped what I was doing. It wasn't pretty. I loved my girls, and I wanted things to change. I got that if anything were to change, it had to start with me. As I became more conscious, I couldn't bear the thought that I had caused so much suffering for my daughters. How could I not be doing the right thing by them? In addition to these more noble thoughts, my ego was wounded. That damned ego of mine—I didn't want to be seen as anything but a good mother.

The girls had survived the repercussions of my early 1981 three-week stay at Tulane Medical Center and my three-year affair with the priest of their church where chapel took place every day. Or so I thought in my absorbed and oblivious way. Anne Phyfe made sure her world was under control and acted cool as a cucumber, but in the period after the affair, I saw she was hiding other things. Rebecca would go upstairs, lie on her bed, and cover herself for hours under Campbell, her protective, red-lined, blue Campbell Soup quilt, and then float down the long flight of steps underneath it. And Jennifer was exasperatingly clingy each time I walked out the door to yet another meeting, feeling torn as I left her and her sisters with the Honduran housekeeper—but that didn't stop me. On the surface, the girls became proficient at packing up their books and belongings to travel between Tom's apartment and mine. They slogged their way brilliantly through other people's demands on them, no doubt filling their figurative baskets with plenty to reveal to a therapist one day. What was I thinking? My girls. I loved them. But the love was stuffed down deep inside me, frozen—I kept getting an image of a large block of blue ice—and I had yet to learn how to crack it open in order to be able to express that love. That would only come when I learned to look at myself with love. I thank God that Tom was a loving and stable father to them. It would be a while before I even understood what being *present* meant. I was too busy walking the line. Later I realized I wasn't cold and frigid. I was paralyzed in this tension and not yet free to love myself or anyone else.

Separated in the late summer of 1983, free of the affair by late spring 1984, legally divorced in January 1986, struggling in a new half-time job so I could pay the rent without collecting a worker's compensation check—which I subsequently did for almost a year—and responding to my own insights about my destructive behavior, I felt backed into a corner, desperate. I had to take some action toward change, and that's when I got to know my sister Penny better.

I hadn't known Penny well until then, but by that time both of us were divorced and coming to terms with alcohol addiction, and during that struggle we grew closer. During that period, my sister stunned me. Even with her struggles, she seemed to live more freely than I dared. She blasted songs on her radio, singing out loud every word of every song. She was not afraid to laugh out loud in both private and public. And she loved smoking Marlboro Reds and eating fudge. Plus she was the best dancer in the family after my mother and grandmother.

I secretly attended my first Alcoholics Anonymous meeting in a neighborhood far removed from my own. The first time I set foot through the door, I almost guffawed. These were not my people. What was I doing here with a white-haired old man who looked like a drunk and kept scratching his leg, a young-ish man in pale beige work clothes, washed out and smoking Camels nonstop? And that woman with dyed black hair, sequins on her glasses, and tomato-red lipstick? Or the black man who mumbled his hello and couldn't stop talking? But by the end of the meeting, a mellowness had opened up in me. I stayed to play cards with the group, laughing and enjoying myself.

"I'm drinking too much, and my life is out of control," I said to the group when I took a turn to speak. "When I drink, my moods change and my impulsiveness increases, and I don't like the way I act—so judgmental and irascible. And I am learning I have to stay off alcohol so I don't jeopardize the effect of the lithium I take to keep my moods and behaviors in hand." So began my campaign to be responsible and accountable to myself and my daughters. It was time to buckle down and enlist help from a therapist in getting my life in order.

Social skills and people-pleasing tendencies kept me afloat for a while. Soon the meaning of the twelve steps would take over my life, and all that social breeding would become less important. May 12, 1987 was the day of my last drink, the first day of uninterrupted years of taking lithium—I'm still taking it over a quarter century later—and at times could allow in the beginnings of self-discovery and a measure of peace of mind. It struck me as ironic that just as I was discovering things about myself, gaining myself, I was losing my family. And it wasn't only my family I was leaving behind, it was a whole community, a whole way of life. To discover myself would take some space, and I would need to let go of other things—like the comfortable, expected, familiar world of the Garden Study Club.

Two years before Tom and I split up, I had begun feeling overburdened with obligation, some of it self-imposed, some socially expected. One Tuesday afternoon after the divorce, I changed my clothes to dress up for a monthly Garden Study Club meeting. *Oh my God*, I said to myself, *I dread the day when I have to host members here.*

I was flattered to be one of the youngest members, and I liked some of the women, but was this for me? A few of them seemed genuinely interested in their gardens and the state of landscaping and botanical plots in the city. I admired them for that, but I shuddered to think of getting my home spit-and-polish ready for a meeting with other perfection-oriented women. The prospect of membership responsibilities rolled around relentlessly, and despite the juicy things I learned about plants and gardens and the fact that I enjoyed some of the more engaging women in the club, I couldn't sink my teeth into it. Maybe it was just the phase of my life. Or the tension in my traditional life leading to the need to be whole.

"Dear Elizabeth, I have appreciated my time in the Garden Study Club. However, I am writing you as president of the club to resign my membership."

The club president, Elizabeth Keenan, also my neighbor,

called after receiving my letter and said, "You *can't* resign, Marilee. Just take your letter back! That's ridiculous!"

"This is what I want and need to do. Please accept my resignation, Elizabeth."

"I'm not going to do it, Marilee. You know your mother and grandmother would be so upset, and so would everyone in the club. Plus, you'll want the company of this group, if not now, then in the future."

I appreciated that, and the fact that she still wanted me as a member after my affair, but I had ambiguous feelings about these social groups—I couldn't stand to keep score, and uneasiness plagued me when I wondered where I stood with the group. I wanted to be able to plant seeds figuratively and literally without dealing with social trappings and worrying about outcomes.

So even though my resignation wasn't yet accepted, I stopped paying dues and considered myself officially no longer a member of the Garden Study Club—shedding one of the components of my Uptown pedigree. In time, I would grieve some aspects of losing these associations—as predicted by the president—but for the time being, I needed to break out.

Not long after I quit the Garden Study Club, the Junior League, in which I had been active for ten years, hung like an albatross around my neck, although if I had a passion for a project, I could work endlessly on it, as I did in 1979 when I co-chaired the International Year of the Child Committee. I marched with other committee members into the vast and historic Charity Hospital on Tulane Avenue to protest the practice of newborn babies being kept apart from their mothers and not nursed for the first week of their lives. I was stunned and horrified. I had also been passionate about helping abused and recovering women gain job-seeking skills when I led career development workshops for women.

A surprise to myself, I had also liked watering the garden of one of the fundraising Junior League Decorator Show Houses. I stood under trees in the shade and nurtured plants with water, feeling the calming energy of the growth around me. But I realized that many of the considerable number of skills that I gained through diverse volunteer placements and board positions had little to do with what I, Marilee, wanted—not that I had clarity on that—and the various placements had helped me realize what I *didn't* want to do. I had met a number of intelligent and well-meaning women in these ranks, but I had enough on my plate without trying to schedule in activities not fundamentally relevant to my life at that time.

So a year or so after I resigned from the Garden Study Club, I handed in another resignation, this time to the secretary of the Junior League.

"Marilee, I won't take it." Same treatment. "You don't want to give up League membership. Just think! You are about to move from being a regular member to being a sustaining member (over forty). Among other things, you would miss the Mint Julep Sustainers' Tea every spring." She smiled. "Come on, keep this in your life."

I didn't change my mind. I told myself I needed to shed affiliation with this group to make space for myself. It had taken me a decade to realize that I had gone about trying to connect with my history and place in New Orleans, the lifestyle I'd been born to and in which my family had lived for generations, through a sense of noblesse oblige—and I had enjoyed much of it. I had finally grasped it and needed to act on my new understanding. So many of the Junior League activities comprised exactly what had kept me separate from the spaciousness I needed to get to know myself.

Around that time, as I was shedding the role I'd been groomed to play and discovering myself, I decided I needed to visit Ruth Nobles, beloved former family babysitter and cook. I don't know what I was thinking, but in a moment of confused *noblesse oblige*, I bought a twenty-pound turkey as a ticket of admission. I felt a strong link to Ruth, considered her to be my second mother, and wanted to tell her about my three daughters. I wanted to hug her as part of discovering my new life and to reconnect with the best part of the world I felt I was leaving behind. When I knocked on her door, turkey in arms, my entry into her house was stilted. I had interrupted a barefooted and hurried Ruth, busy playing a game of cards with three friends in the rear of her home. It was vexing and embarrassing to walk in there and realize I was intruding. I hadn't called ahead; I hadn't thought this through. I had thought only about myself and my needs.

"Marilee," said Ruth, pushing me toward the door, her ruffled party dress swishing, "go talk with Cynthia in the living room—she's in town from California—I'll come back out after my game," and she shuffled barefoot back to her cards.

In effect, Ruth had her own clubs and Junior League equivalents, something I hadn't fully grasped. I was discovering a whole life that this person already had in her own world that I hadn't realized, because I had seen Ruth only in her role at our house and not as a person. Later I realized that this was important to me because I too wanted to be seen as a person, not the role carved out for me.

I regrouped, put on a smile, and said, "Of course, Ruth."

Cynthia Meadoux, reclining on the sofa, laughed. "You know, Mama says you and Pixie and Penny are her white children." I heard an edge in Cynthia's voice, and it pierced my shaky sense of ease. I felt it in the middle of my chest just above my stomach. I felt profoundly uncomfortable, pure and simple. I said nothing, shrinking into my sweater—I hadn't expected to see her. Cynthia was Ruth's second living daughter, Esther's younger sister, and lived near Los Angeles with her husband and children. Ruth's oldest daughter, Bebe, had moved to Chicago in the 1950s, borne two children, and died of cancer by the age of thirty.

I was struggling to figure out how to make my way in my own clan, and I hadn't a clue how to have an honest interchange with people of color who were neither working for my family nor for one of my friend's families. I guessed that blacks couldn't be their true selves in the white world and so had to hold two realities together at once—what the white world expected of them and who they really were. Was this similar to what I needed to learn—how to move through that royalty world I'd been thrown into but be myself? Similar maybe, but not the same. Ruth had her own world, a world I didn't understand and maybe never could. But one difference I could see: Ruth liked her Mardi Gras clubs and felt at home in them, and I didn't feel at home in mine. The clubs worked differently for the two of us. My closed Uptown structure of knowing blasted open. I had no friends of color, knew only graduates of private white schools, and when I began to question the dualism I'd grown up in, my mind clouded—it was too much to take in. My real self had no practice in seeing beyond myself. Was my visit to Ruth ingenuously motivated by a false platform of *noblesse oblige*? Ouch. I didn't fit in here anymore than I did anywhere else at that point. I stood still for a minute, my heart racing, I had stepped so far out of my comfort zone.

I conversed with Cynthia for a minute or two. I still detected an edge to her voice underneath the niceties we exchanged—ages of her children, her husband's name, her work with Hollywood entertainers—and I left before my anxiety got the better of me. What would it have been like if I had plopped myself on the sofa with her and asked her one question after another about her existence—about moving away from New Orleans, how she felt about her mother taking care of white girls, how she felt about her life? This visit to Ruth taught me that the power structure upon which our relationship was built was not operative in her house.

My role-bound, masked self, devoted to the Junior League, Garden Study Club, Mardi Gras drill, and, of course, raising three daughters, was waking up to the reality that I had been living in a make-believe world and that my recent attempts to break free from it had been feeble at best.

Chapter 13

THE WHITE HANDKERCHIEF

I n 1986, I ran into Ed James at a Crutcher-Tufts company holiday party in New Orleans. Ed was a business friend of my stepfather, Crutcher, and I'd met him years before at my parents' house when I was a young married woman. At the party I spotted Ed talking to Crutcher's partner, J. D., and I approached them to say hello. Mr. James's hair had turned from brown to silver since I had last seen him, and his large blue eyes behind thick lenses were warm and friendly. "Hello, Mr. James," I said. "Hi, J. D."

"Oh, please call me Ed," he said, smiling widely.

J. D. patted my shoulder and veered off toward the bar, leaving us to talk.

I learned that Ed was in the process of divorce from his second wife, and he seemed to know I had just gone through my own. We each sipped on our drinks, mine a ginger ale. We moved on to talking about books. "I just finished Jean Auel's novel *The Clan of the Cave Bear.* A resourceful woman takes over the leadership of her clan—a great story about life in the cave-man era."

"I've heard about it," he said. "I'll read it on your recommendation. I'm about to finish an odd and bizarre book named *Perfume* by Patrick Süskind. It's the story of a murderer whose obsession with his sense of smell leads him to kill. Fascinating, the workings of the human mind. But tell me what you're doing."

"I've worked on a couple of local women's rights events, and I say a gratitude prayer every time January 22 rolls around to honor Roe v. Wade."

"It's a real feat that it was passed—amazing and welcome," Ed said. "So would you say you're a feminist?"

I nodded firmly and told him about working on local gatherings for Women's Caucus for Art and the River Meeting, and my partnering job with another woman to produce the Working Women's Forum though Newcomb College. "No marching yet!" I said. "But, yes. I *am* a feminist, although lately I've focused more on just keeping my family going while I work. How about you? Are you a feminist?"

"I would have to say yes."

I was curious and attracted to this calm older man, to his openness to feminism, the merry blue eyes obscured by his thick eyeglasses, and our lively conversation. We danced together, and the rest of the roomful of people in cocktail garb standing with drinks in hand receded. I felt as if we were the only ones on the floor. Several months later, I received a package from him containing the book *Perfume*. His gift was so out of the blue. Did his sending it mean something? Was he thinking about me? I called to thank him and felt naughty and bold making the call and speaking with him. Then silence again. I told myself he's busy, completing his divorce, not interested.

Three years later, in late 1989, Ed sold his Houston company and moved to New Orleans to consult with Crutcher-Tufts. I sat next to him at my cousin's New Year's Eve coming-out dinner at Mr. B's Restaurant and remembered our conversation and dance. I wanted to get to know this man—he was different—foreign, Western, not a New Orleanian! I thought maybe he had a shy gene. I noticed a couple of times while telling a story, he wouldn't look at me. Instead, he'd look straight at the person on my right. And sometimes, while talking with one person, he'd look at the person next to her or him. I found this tendency slightly unsettling at first. But his thinking was right, and his values a refreshing change from the royal court of New Orleans men. He didn't dramatize. He spoke evenly, logically, and cited facts that made sense, given his background. He'd trained as a chemist at San Jose State College and then, after working for Shell a short time, the company had awarded him a fellowship to Stanford. He'd studied for a master's degree in petroleum engineering, left to serve in the army for a year in the Pacific, come home to complete his degree, and then worked for Shell for twenty-five years—including a year in The Hague.

Ed and Crutcher had met while Ed was working for Lehmann Brothers in New York in its Oil and Gas Department. Way back when, they'd joined together to do oil and gas deals, Ed providing his engineering and financial expertise. Before moving to New Orleans, he had run a small oil company in Calgary, Canada, for several years before moving it to Houston.

When Ed and I sat next to each other at my cousin's debut party, that spark I remembered was still there. A few months after the December 1990 party, Ed and I ran into each other at an Uptown grocery store. I had to nudge Ed into going out, and I did. We made a date to see a movie, and began seeing each other, oh, so slowly, nothing like the hasty involvements of my past. I liked his kindness, his brain, humor, steadiness, the way he listened to me, and his quietly sexy nature and looks—I was drawn to him. And he recognized me as myself, which I felt I hadn't experienced in my New Orleans world.

In the fall of that year, just beginning to date and travel with Ed, I entered the graduate program at the Tulane School of Social Work. I'd clamped onto the once-shelved idea when I had realized priesthood was not for me. Or I for it. I had learned that people with bipolar disorder can get super religious and hyperfocused. That was me. And I mustered courage to pursue a career. Now I felt ready. Social work would give me the skills, practice, and credentials to counsel people, as well as a career for myself—a check to live on—and provide me with a rationale for sharing information on living skills. True, part of my interest was a genuine desire to help people be better people, but part, no doubt, was a projection of my needs to figure out my life—or avoid it by concentrating on others.

Things between Ed and me picked up fast. That first fall, we visited the San Juan Islands in the Pacific Northwest, where we were joined by his sons Stephen and then Regan and his family. A few weeks later, we flew east to be present at Stephen's ceremony at Boston University. In December we traveled to Santa Fe for a white Christmas with side trips to Los Alamos and Abiquiú, where Georgia O'Keeffe painted red rocks. Back home in New Orleans, when we weren't traveling, we went to movies, discussed books, walked in Audubon Park, and ate dinners he cooked while watching *Masterpiece Theater* in his apartment. I liked this man, found him to be bright, trustworthy, straightforward—and comfortable to be with. I didn't realize how much I liked him until one evening at the end of our first year of going together. We were having drinks at a wedding reception, and a woman a little older than I came up and started flirting with Ed. I went taut and felt my chest inflate. I don't remember my exact words, but I am certain that my body language signaled *Red flag! Red flag!* Fear of losing my man! Ed was oblivious, just talking away with this attractive woman, until I took him by the arm and guided him to the opposite corner of the room, stunned at my own reaction.

Ed had a way of bringing out deep emotions in me and welcoming them. During our Boston trip for Ed's son's doctoral graduation, we drove to McLean, twenty-five miles away in Belmont, where I had spent pretty much the whole of what would have been my sophomore year of college. Ed parked the car near Belknap II, the ward I had lived on. He turned off the ignition, and as he turned his head toward me, all the tears I'd amassed about my unexpected Wellesley leave-taking in September 1961 and my entry into the hospital spilled down the front of my sweater and soaked into my blouse and bra. They took me completely by surprise. I crumpled over in the seat next to Ed. I didn't even know how I got there. A fleeting thought dropped in—I can't do this to Ed—but the tears kept coming anyway. When I reached for him, he took me sideways in his arms, no alarm in his face. Quiet and receiving, he held my wracked body—his shirt blotting some of my deluge. He didn't say, "Now, now, stop crying, it's okay." He didn't push me away or make fun of my emotional outburst. Had I ever encountered anyone who could be a container for my emotions like this? I felt met.

Once my tears had subsided and my body had stopped shaking, we climbed out of the car to walk around. Tears streamed down my cheeks again. Grief and shame flowed through my cells—so much had transpired in so little time here. I slobbered away but couldn't find my Kleenex. Then my white knight pulled out his white handkerchief, and I took it and wiped my nose with it, feeling relief and closure. I was in love.

A few quiet minutes passed. Stillness. I sat up straight, took a deep breath, and realized I no longer needed to dwell on all I'd missed at Wellesley and my experience at McLean. We walked back to the car, the strength of my released emotions eclipsed by Ed's acceptance of me. We had not been seeing each other for long, just a few months, but I knew without a doubt that he had passed some unnamed test and proved himself a worthy partner. It felt as if he had received my being. Already I loved his curiosity, the way he read *The Wall Street Journal* and *The New York Times* every morning and consumed countless novels and history books. I admired his sense of fairness and that he was more content staying home and reading a good book than going to a cocktail party. When the topic of religion came up, he made it clear that he was in awe of the universe and amazed at the way things work, but not a believer. A fifty-year oil business dinosaur—analyst, financier, and problem solver—he also excelled as a chef, poring over recipes, standing over the kitchen counter nailing flavors from Louisianian, Moroccan, Indian, French, Mongolian, and Mexican cuisines. He told good stories, quoted Shakespeare and Lewis Carroll, and sang verses from *The Mikado*. My ginger cat liked him too. He plopped himself in Ed's lap the minute he walked through my door.

But at that moment on the McLean campus, I was filled with gratitude for the safe container Ed created by being his calm, bright, and brainy self. His sweet, loving, masculine energy attracted me.

"Do you want to stay at McLean a little longer?" he asked.

"No," I said. "This is enough. I've come a long way, though in some ways not, but I've made peace with my time here." I told him how my mother had called me here and announced that I would be Queen of the Osiris Ball and make my debut, and how I had flown from Boston to New Orleans for that whirlwind of Mardi Gras. He shook his head in disbelief and held me tighter.

Chapter 14

DEBUTS IN
OTHER KEYS

Each of my three daughters decided not to make her debut in the Mardi Gras tradition.

Not long after my oldest daughter, Anne Phyfe, stepped off the plane from her freshman year at the University of Vermont, a year younger than I was when I entered McLean, she and her father and I plopped down on sofas in my apartment living room. A dense spring rain poured down outside the window that was cracked open, and the heady fragrance of sweet olive settled into the room. It was 1990, the year I started dating Ed and seven years since the separation and later divorce, and I felt a familiar stiffness whenever Tom and I were in a room together, a feeling that would improve with time.

"Anne Phyfe," Tom said, "it's decision-making time. Where are you about making your debut?"

"Oh, you guys," she said evenly, pushing back her long, straight hair behind her ear. "I love you, but I can't imagine doing that. Thank you for offering this, but I want to focus on my English and women's studies at UVM and spend my junior year in England." She fingered the buckle on one of her modern clunky shoes. "I know Mom and my aunts all made their debuts, but I can't see doing it."

"Are you certain you'd rather not?"

Anne Phyfe shook her head, "No, Mom and Dad, I don't want to make my debut."

I simultaneously felt relief and nostalgia—relief considering my misgivings about the whole Carnival system and nostalgia remembering how I felt cherished when my father walked me across the floor at Momus, and when, as a queen, I'd bowed to my mother and grandmother. I felt a bit guilty at being let off the hook as mother of the debutante by Anne Phyfe's decision—and free. It was unbelievable to me that she could make such a choice and not feel she had to live up to social expectations—thinking for herself, unlike my predicament three decades earlier when it had never occurred to me that I could do something different. I also felt a strong pull toward family and tradition.

I wondered whether Anne Phyfe just didn't want to spend so much time in New Orleans for a number of reasons, or if she simply wasn't interested in a debut. Or was she simply coming from another perspective? Did she intuit that I was not totally available for the job of being mother of a deb—grappling with holding my life together in the midst of being newly sober, attending frequent twelve-step meetings, sticking to my meds, working at the moment for the Institute for Human Understanding and part time for Planned Parenthood of Louisiana. Not to mention taking two psychology courses so I could apply for graduate social work school. I needed a bona fide career, and social work came up as the one most consonant with my interests. I had told myself I would be willing to go through with Anne Phyfe's debut if she wanted it, but I felt a wave of relief that I wouldn't have to juggle that ball, no pun intended, along with others; it would have been exhausting. I also acknowledged that I had been excited that she was breaking free of the system. And a little worried. What would the social repercussions be whenever she returned to New Orleans? But I ultimately chose not to worry about that. Some of her high school friends thought she was crazy not to do this. For them, it was a natural part of growing up in New Orleans.

My mother couldn't wrap her head around the news that her oldest granddaughter didn't want to make her debut. "Anne Phyfe," she'd said, "you are being rash, and you might regret this."

"Mimi," Anne Phyfe said, "you're so sweet. It must sound strange for me to turn this down, but I've been gone from New Orleans for a couple of years now, and I see my life away from here. I'll get a lot more out of going to England for the school year than coming home from Vermont a few times to be a debutante."

"I really think this is something you ought to do," Mimi said. "I can't imagine a granddaughter of mine not making her debut. After all, New Orleans is your true home. And besides, I had always planned to give you a tea."

Tom and I had anticipated my mother's reaction. While Anne Phyfe couldn't have been clearer about her stand on the matter, my mother talked to her as if she hadn't heard what Anne Phyfe was saying. I got on the phone and reminded Mom that she had other grandchildren coming up to fulfill her dreams.

So, there was to be no "season" for Anne Phyfe. Still, her godmother Betsy Nalty managed to sneak in a festive and elegant luncheon at Antoine's Restaurant in Anne Phyfe's honor. Anne Phyfe's sisters, female cousins, young women friends, her stepmother, Mom, and I were all dressed up and present sitting around a long table in the Rex room where her great-grandfather's photo hung on the wall along with photographic portraits of all the other men who had reigned as Rex. *Pompano en papil-lote* topped with crabmeat, Antoine's delicious green salad, and a large flaming baked Alaska with Anne Phyfe's name written on it prompted sighs of delight and satisfaction.

"This was just the perfect party, Betsy. Just enough for me," Anne Phyfe said, and off she flew for her junior semester in England. I marveled that compromise had won out and that there was a way out of the tension of family/tradition and self.

I can't remember how it came about that Rebecca chose not to make her debut, but I recall surprise among her old Trinity School friends and no ripple of interest from her Ben Franklin High School friends. Mimi just shook her head. Maybe her aunts talked behind our backs. I felt as if I'd been given another reprieve; it seemed like a sign of the true freedom possible in this situation. In spite of the warnings of a Southern friend who said we'd never see Rebecca again if she went to school outside the South, she flew off to Wesleyan University in Connecticut, a complete switch from the New Orleans scene, and majored in fine arts, focused on tight and meaningful relationships, and spent a junior year painting in Rome. I marveled at the freedom and cleanness of her decision. My friend was wrong. Rebecca returned to New Orleans. And it took her a long time, maybe a couple of years, to reacclimatize to the Big Easy after living among a closely formed academic clan of bright, purpose-ful people. I remember sensing she seemed at first to be on the wrong planet; however, Rebecca came home to New Orleans with well-formed opinions about social justice and a curiosity and passion for her birth city. I had much to learn from her gift of imagining other possibilities.

She reveled in the mixing of media, engagement with other people, the production of pieces, and, after co-directing another documentary and working on other New Orleans-based films, started to create her own film that came to be *By Invitation Only*. Maybe the seeds of that film were sown as curiosity about the traditions she had decided to forego and the exclusionary policies that were entrenched in the Carnival season, inherent in the city's culture.

Her film followed a young debutante who reigned as queen of one of the old-line white balls. In the making of the film, Rebecca became aware or conscious of the social and racial hierarchy that underscored the whole Mardi Gras system. Her African-American boyfriend, Isaac Webb, was not welcome to the balls that she filmed. While she delved into Mardi Gras by following and filming a young white debutante queen during her deb year, she became more and more infuriated at the lines drawn, the arrogant whiteness, the obvious and sometimes unconscious and subtle ways that the men in white organizations looked down on the blacks.

Rebecca brought Isaac for dinner with Ed, Penny, and me at our Amethyst house at the lakefront. Rebecca had told me she wanted me to meet him, the filmmaker she'd collaborated with on another documentary and with whom she had fallen in love. Ed was delighted whenever Rebecca came over, and we liked hearing about the documentaries she worked on. The five of us enjoyed a lark of an evening around our table, happily engaged in conversation punctuated with much laughter, storytelling, and Ed's delectable gumbo. Late in the evening, after Penny had left and Ed had retired, Isaac, Rebecca, and I sat around talking about writing, and he strongly encouraged me to work on the stories I'd been jotting down about New Orleans and Biloxi—I had started writing again after the shock of throwing my journals into the garbage truck.

"Tell your stories out loud," he said. "It's a great way to capture your voice, and then type the recordings and work from that draft." I thought he was looking for an easy way for me to put down the stories, but he reminded me that storytelling had started as an oral tradition.

The evening was a turning point for me in two ways: first, hosting an African-American man for dinner, and then taking in that my daughter was in an interracial relationship. I wanted it to be all right—and I was not of the mind or in a place to lecture about the difficulties they might have in the future, but it was new ground for me. After all, what did I know of such things? I later gratefully recalled how inspired and motivated I was to write because of my conversation with Isaac.

One day in New Orleans, Pixie, Penny, and I were having lunch with our mother at Figaro's on Maple Street. We talked about anything that we remotely had in common, mostly about other members of the family, although Mom and Pixie, two excellent golfers, talked country club golf for a good while first.

Pixie turned to me and said, "Tell me about Rebecca's boyfriend."

"For starters," I said, "Isaac's black, and—" Then I remembered that Mom was sitting with us, and as far as I knew, didn't know anything about him. She sat quietly, face impassive, listening as if nothing unusual were being discussed. I felt upset with myself for talking out of school—this was Rebecca's story to tell—and being the one to inform her grandmother about her relationship. I had never thought to bring it up to Mom. In other words, I had probably avoided the subject. Then I woke up and realized of course Mom has opinions and feelings about this; her silence spoke volumes. I noticed her lips thinning out, an impassive look on her face. I wondered what she was really thinking.

In January of 2001, Rebecca called me and said in an excited voice, "Mimi invited me to tea. She wants to talk to me about something." She loved her grandmother and looked forward to seeing her. The date came. Rebecca and Mimi talked, exchanged stories, and drank tea for quite a while, until Rebecca finally asked, "You mentioned there was something you wanted to talk about?"

Mom began to explain that she hadn't been able to accept Rebecca's relationship with a black man, and she expressed concern about Rebecca's future if they stayed together. "Rebecca," she said to her, "he wouldn't be welcome at the country club."

Mom was fine going to a social engagement with black people, and had done that all over the United States, on golf trips, but when it came to her family and being in New Orleans, it seemed to be another question.

Rebecca called me weeping on the phone. "Mimi is missing out on the most beautiful person I know." She and Isaac were actually on the verge of breaking up after three years together, but she hadn't brought that up to Mom. "I was walking out of the house, down the steps from the front porch, and got a jolt. It hit me. It was the first time I wanted Isaac and me to make it for some other reason beyond the two of us and our love. I wanted us to make it as a political act, too."

Rebecca and Isaac's relationship ended not long after that visit to Mimi's, but they remained friends. I only heard about him through Rebecca. He showed up in *By Invitation Only*, which premiered within several months after Mimi's death in 2006. A second of my daughters had an entirely different set of ideas about what she wanted to do with her life. How could I fight that?

⌒〰

"Debut? I don't have time for that," Jennifer said. By the time it came to our youngest daughter, neither Tom nor I were fazed by her decision. Tom had resigned from at least one krewe by that time. My mother must have expected this decision, because she remained quiet. Some of Jennifer's friends from McGehee

School made their debuts, but not all of them, and only one of her new Lakefront neighborhood friends followed suit. Ed had wondered what all the fuss was back when Anne Phyfe said no, so he just shrugged his shoulders in response; he didn't understand the whole debut and Carnival business anyway.

Jennifer attended McGehee School and went her own way, but in a different fashion. When Jennifer moved with Ed and me to the Lakefront neighborhood house we had rented in 1992, she had no curfew. I didn't think she needed one and wasn't aware that her current forte was sneaking back into the house by climbing over a ground floor bedroom windowsill while we were asleep. When her friends came over to spend the night, they got away with stealing out to party while their parents thought they were safe and sound at our house—and Ed and I slept deeply just thirty feet away. The girls drove off—car motors quiet, headlights off—to the end of the street, around the corner, and then switched on their headlights, and headed to Parlay's, a well-known neighborhood Irish pub. I couldn't believe that all this went on right under my nose, but Jennifer liked to party with her friends. Later, while writing this book, I realized my concern that she was being a bit wild stemmed from my own experience of being a pro at stealing out of the Walnut Street apartment when I was sixteen.

In January 1997, Jennifer transferred from LSU to Our Lady of Holy Cross College, a small Catholic college across the river on the West Bank in Algiers where her boyfriend Danny was taking classes. She was too busy with her work and play to say yes to a debut, and none of her friends were involved in the Uptown scene. She earned a bachelor of science degree in elementary education and threw her cap in the air with other graduates, then immediately dived into a public school teaching job.

A couple of months after she and Danny got engaged, Jennifer, now twenty-four, paid me an impromptu visit, bursting through our kitchen door without looking me in the eye, curled up in fetal fashion on the red slip-covered sofa, and bawled non-stop for thirty minutes. I suspected that was easier than telling me whatever in the world was going on. In bits and snatches, she said, "I can't marry Danny. I'm not in love with him. It wouldn't work."

I kept quiet and listened, but I was stunned. I thought about how Danny was already like a son-in-law to me after seven years. He was sweet, slow, and steady. I was used to him. *She's wearing his ring, for God's sake.* The engagement party had already taken place, and wedding invitations were printed. The reservation at the riverfront reception venue would have to be cancelled. *Damn!*

Then sniveling, an hour after her grand entrance, she sat up and said, "There's someone else."

Long silence.

"I really love him."

Silence. I waited.

"His name is Chris, and I met him through my friend after Danny and I became engaged." The words tumbled out of her mouth. "He's divorced. He has two daughters, eight and six. They live on the West Bank in Algiers, a couple of corners away from Our Lady of Holy Cross. The family's name is Arnone."

"All right, Jennifer, I hear you. Let's just sit here for a bit." I had my hand on her back.

She cried a little more, then talked about falling for Chris on the dock at the lake at a friend's family's picnic. Fifteen minutes later, Jennifer and I were laughing, and I could detect an aliveness in her that I loved to see.

A year later—Jennifer told Chris they had to wait a year—Chris proposed. And so, Jennifer moved lock, stock, and barrel into the arms of the fun-loving, expressive, and generous Italian-Irish Roman Catholic Arnone family in Algiers, Louisiana. It wasn't that easy, probably one of the hardest years of her life. She was learning how to be a parent to Chris's two daughters at the same time she had lost many friends because of the breakup with Danny.

Jennifer and I collaborated on plans for the wedding, and they were married at Holy Name of Mary Catholic Church on Algiers Point in the presence of three hundred people in a traditional wedding ceremony officiated by Chris's brother, a Catholic priest. She wore a beautiful simple ivory-white, custom-made wedding dress—for my pleasure in the giving of it and working with her and the dressmaker to design it. After all, this was her real debut! My sibs and parents came, and local friends attended and huddled together in the midst of all the fun. I did a stellar job as mother of the bride—right up until the moment that I had to take off my two-inch heels because my feet were in such pain from dancing so long at Rosie's Jazz Hall!

A picture of the Pope with a blessing for their first child adorned the Arnones' upstairs hall. It had been brought back from Rome by Chris's brother, John Arnone, a Catholic priest, giving me some pause; I was so steeped in a background with Episcopalians and Presbyterians. It seemed as if Jennifer would wear that cloak loosely, and what could I do? I quickly and easily loved Chris—a third-generation firefighter with a strong artistic gift for decorating his home, designing and executing settings for Mardi Gras balls, taking care of his family, cooking red beans and rice, and a talent for cooking up pounds and pounds of boiled crawfish and corn and potatoes and spreading them out on large tables covered in newspapers in his and Jennifer's backyard to feed their family and friends—in the traditional New Orleans way.

Watching my girls turn down the 150-year ritual of making a debut was an unexpected gift. They taught me, one after another, that my old narrative of tension between family/social expectations was passé, unnecessary, and certainly didn't resonate with my girls—a whole new ballgame was possible now.

Or was for them. If I would only learn from them, my precious, self-possessed daughters! I literally felt like a cap had been lifted off—an invisible cap that weighed down on my brain— that represented following rituals that did not align with the human in me, my human spirit. A new direction.

Chapter 15

THE ⌢BOXER

W hile my girls were discovering possibilities for their lives and creating their own debuts, I was discovering new possibilities for myself. Since 1987, I had focused on the twelve steps—in AA, Al-Anon, ACOA, and most reluctantly, Overeaters Anonymous—completing my master's in social work in December 1991, and keeping up with my girls as best I could. After graduation, I worked at the Jefferson Parish Human Services Authority in Metairie, a New Orleans suburb, as a clinical social worker with a range of clients from children and adolescents to adult men and women. I witnessed people with personality quirks and distorted thinking, self-inflated and self-deflated views of themselves, tactics that helped them survive in their lives but that no longer served them. Their skewed thinking contributed to addictive practices—substance abuse, domestic violence, gambling, and drug dealing. I also worked with people affected by someone else's addiction.

Sometime in 1993, a year after Ed and I moved in together and blended our libraries, furniture, art, linens, tools, and cookware in our house near the lake, I felt a need to embark on a regular workout program but wasn't eager to pick up a tennis racket again. I did so much sitting on the job, my body was going crazy. That's when I followed my OA friends to a boxing gym, owned and managed by one John Carmody from Australia. Ed was amused and watched me go my way. Jennifer wailed, "Oh, Mom," embarrassed that her mother would go to a boxing gym of all things. Twenty years later she probably wouldn't have been so repelled. I never heard about it from the other two girls when I wrote them. I learned later that John Carmody had been in recovery himself and engaged in twelve-step programs since the early 1970s, which he talked about freely, using his experience to help others. As time passed, I learned that as a psychiatric nurse in the Outback, he had introduced forensic and correctional programs into state facilities. He had extensive experience with substance abuse, mental health, eating disorders, anger management, trauma recovery, and family system recovery services. At his gym in New Orleans, he offered amateur boxing training for all ages, support for professional boxers, and therapeutic services.

Sometime in my second year of working out at John's gym, around 1994 or 1995, I grew restless to do something other than the repetitive exercises of hitting into a sparring partner's receiving gloves one-two-one-two-one-two or rhythmically hitting the little ball dangling from an overhead board. It was time for me to suit up to box with John in the ring. The quirky owner and head trainer, whose ears resembled Mister Spock's, had many roles, including mentor to many—from top boxers to the amateur women from twelve-step programs who were drawn to his gym. I had been one of them.

When I made the decision to go into the ring with John, I felt so weak it scared me. I needed to shake up my energy or I'd go bonkers. I might as well give up. That particular day, I donned the women's red-and-black leather breastplate—a big, old red smelly thing—nothing like the pointed sexy ones worn by Madonna. I inserted my mouthguard, tightened my shoe-laces, wound blue cotton wraps round and round my hands, and stood still while another student boxer tied the laces on my gloves for me. The worst part was putting on the wet, stinking helmet already worn by half a dozen dripping, reeking others—a true sign of my resolve. I stretched my hamstrings against the hard edge of the ring and waited my turn while watching two others spar.

John's ring assistant came to get me. "You're up. Go in there and get him now. Stab him right in the gut—if he'll let you."

I nodded and climbed the three steps onto the outside of the ring. I lifted the ropes and swung my left leg, then my right underneath. I was in. John stood on the opposite side of the ring finishing up with a man, drenched in sweat, who had just sparred with him. The man lifted the ropes to leave the ring. Then John turned toward me, only slightly sweaty and crackling with energy.

"You think yer ready, eh? You think yer going to get up enough guts to come in here and hit me, do ya? C'mon lassie," he goaded me in his Aussie English.

Before I knew it, he gave me the high five of boxing, holding his gloves to mine, a sign of respect and equality that seemed to mock me that day.

He peppered my arm with mini-punches, then my ribs, and my back near my kidneys. How could he come at me so fast? His feet danced so quickly I could feel the pressure, even when he didn't touch me. I tumbled backward, collapsing into the ropes, pissed and helpless. *I chose this*, I told myself, breathless. *Oh, no, if I get caught in the ropes I'll never get up*, I thought.

"Move it, girl. You're being weak. Where's your gumption?" That word gumption triggered an explosion of energy in me.

John kept going at me, and before I knew it, I did the impossible. I drew myself up from my abs and pounded on him with every ounce of my strength.

I savored the charge of energy. I danced from side to side and grinned inside. Then I consciously pummeled John for each man who had disappointed me, loud grunts punctuating each hit. I called on energies dormant for decades. I fought back on this man who represented so many men that I had gone unconscious with. When I suddenly realized how much physical and mental power was wrapped up in thinking of these men as jerks, I experienced a shift. I no longer had to relegate myself to the ropes. I moved with purpose. Perspiration flooded my eyes and rolled down my cheeks, my back, and between my breasts under the stinky breastplate. I smelled my own sweat through the stench and rejoiced. I felt triumphant! I experienced the gift of fighting back and letting go.

In 1997, after five years at the clinic experiencing the ecstasy and tribulations of being a clinical social worker to people in various stages of oblivion, struggle, and growth, and becoming an integral part of the addictions staff family at the Human Services Authority, I began working as a supervisor. Thankfully, during that time I worked with a therapist who facilitated insights into my own healing. She helped me clear up at least some of the distortions in the way I saw clients so I could respond professionally and be of service to them.

One day, just as I finished a session with a clinic client, the executive director of the authority, Leslie Tremaine, knocked on my door and entered to speak with me. She sat up straight on the two-seat sofa facing the door, and I slid into a chair with my bookshelf at my back.

"Marilee," she said, "we have a huge need here in the parish to address the troubles of adolescents entering the juvenile justice system so early." She filled me in on the statistics and shared her regret about how little was being done in the system for these boys. I wondered why in the world she was telling me this. We had never had a sit-down talk before. True, I had co-led several adolescent groups and had an affinity for this age group—no doubt because I was not very far from my own adolescent phase of development! I knew from working with them a mere hour or two a week that we'd been able to scratch the surface in facilitating a shift in the way they viewed themselves and the world. Maybe my supervisor had mentioned my work to her.

The director and I continued our discussion during the next couple of days and found ourselves in agreement that a key ingredient to working with this age group would be to create an environment of unconditional love punctuated with firm limits, where the young clients had a chance to learn social skills and self-discipline in a setting in which they could experience being heard and treated with respect.

Leslie then asked, "Would you be interested in developing such a program?" A little panic boiled in my belly. *Could I run a program with so much at stake? Interrupt the nice life I was developing?* But I was intrigued—wouldn't it be neat to be part of having an impact on these boys' young lives? As she talked, I felt my heart expand in gratitude for her vision of hope and love— such a gift in a clinical setting where behavior was often labeled and analyzed to death. I thought about the offer over the following week. What could I bring to such a program? I talked with my supervisor about the logistics of clinic cases I would have to transfer or close—some with regret. Every hour of the day, I contemplated what vehicle could serve this goal.

One night soon after, I woke at three o'clock with a big *aha!* Of course! Talk to John! The perfect person—with fascinating experience and passionate about helping young people in trouble. By that time, I had been going to his gym for a couple of years and had had that demanding experience in the ring that ranked as an initiation into a new level of consciousness, and I figured John would be the ideal person to consult about developing a program. Maybe he'd even be interested in being involved. This might be a great collaboration. I liked his energy, even though it could overwhelm me. There were times it was difficult to hold my own ground around him; I still had trouble grounding myself fifteen years after Suzanne Lacy's comment, "Marilee, you are not grounded!" But I had the administrative backing, clinical skills, and enthusiasm for learning more.

I walked into John's gym in street clothes a couple of days later and met with him to discuss my idea. Two hours later we left his office, filled with zeal for what we had come up with—a plan that used our combined abilities and talents. I wrote up a proposal and passed it by the director, and after a few items were addressed—funding, staff, transportation, source of the boys, proper clothes and equipment for the boys, John's contract, drug screens, and family meeting space—we were off and running. I wonder if I would have started in with this next phase of my social work career if I hadn't gone through the stinky breastplate initiation in the ring.

Thus was born our adolescent boxing program. Fifteen boys at a time came to John's gym and my agency's clinic for family meetings. At the beginning of each, I was stunned by what I saw—the boys had no idea how to behave. They stood around the gym, poking each other, talking loudly in crude language, brashly getting in each other's way, interrupting conversations, and heading straight for pairs of gloves hanging on hooks. They stuck their hands in them, and randomly started punching their friends.

"Okay, laddies," John said at the beginning of each program. "You'll do everything proper before you ever get into the ring. Every day you practice." Some of the boys stood, arms crossed. Some sat as if they had no energy whatsoever. A few leaned against the old posts in the barn of a gym.

In a firm, even voice, John explained the protocol. Never standing still, he spoke to the boys. (I found out later he had ADHD, which might have explained his amazingly high energy.) "You tie your shoes properly. You take a pair of long blue wraps, and this is how you wind them around your hands and tuck them in proper to protect them." He held a pair of gloves up high.

"Then you can put on your gloves, and this is how you tie the long laces. Get help from a buddy if you need it." He turned to his assistant, who tied the loose ends on the gloves. And I remember him saying, "And, no," a slow smile easing across his face, "you can't wear pants hanging off your butts in the ring." Sullen looks on a couple of boys' faces. "You need proper boxing shorts, and you'll be given some." He reached in his pocket and held up a piece of cloth. "And one of our gym's special shirts to tuck in your shorts." He smiled widely. "I tolerate no filthy language. Respect each other and the staff and the other people training in the gym."

On the multiple occasions that a boy made a gender-based slur, John would stop everything and express to the group present that sexual harassment would not be tolerated, either. We trained the staff to do the same. The staff was trained to act with dignity, treat the boys with respect, speak eye to eye, offer encouragement, and praise every step taken. The boys learned quickly to look up to John and show courtesy to staff. Manners in the gym, manners in the family meetings, manners in the ring—by the end of three months, the graduates were unrecognizable as the boys we'd seen on the first day.

John enlisted the help of a boxing regular and friend at the gym to fund suppers for the fifteen boys at the famous Mother's Restaurant on Poydras Street. We'd walk in a unit down the sidewalk five blocks from the gym to the restaurant. The boys not only got a good meal New Orleans style—seafood platter, corned beef and cabbage, red beans and rice, fried chicken, white bean soup, turtle soup—but they learned manners as well. They learned where forks and knives and spoons were set on the table, where napkins were positioned and then placed in their laps. They sat up straight with feet under the table, learned respect for wait staff, how to make conversation, how to be ready to go on an interview appropriately—all part of becoming productive members of society.

One day, John and I sat on a wooden platform high above the gym, planning details of the program. Our chairs were about six feet apart. As we talked, he leaned over and touched my arm—in exactly the way he did with everyone—making a point, nothing more. But neediness can be a great distorter. Suddenly, impulsively, I said something about what I considered was going on between us—something I felt carnally from that marvelous and, for me, tricky second chakra. And John said something to the effect of, "Oh, no, no, no, Marilee." He reared back in his chair. Then he leaned forward earnestly. "That is not what we're about." I felt like hiding under my seat. John continued, something like, "We have a fantastic partnership working together for these lads. We each have amazing talents that complement the other, but don't let yourself go beyond that, lassie. You're just needy today. Get a good night's sleep! I have a loving relationship with my partner. You have that lovely man, Ed. Let's go for a healthy connection—let go of this fleeting desire to merge with what you think I am."

He was spot on. I must have been ready to hear him, and I miraculously allowed myself to recalibrate right then and there. I was embarrassed, and he, this eccentric psychiatric nurse from the Outback, was kind about it. I allowed myself to grasp what he was talking about. We sat there across from each other on the elevated platform, and I emitted a long breath. We agreed to meet again in two days and continue our planning. I went home chastened and relieved and grateful for what John had to say, if still embarrassed. Ouch! I actually felt hopeful. Illusion so quickly dismissed! Dismantled before my eyes. What a gift!

Ouch! again. Reflecting back, I had repeated history. Another such incident occurred when I was just divorced in 1986, part-time development staff at a nonprofit counseling center. I was needy enough then to delude myself into thinking that I had attracted one of the principals on the counseling staff. I can see him sitting behind his big desk like a cozy teddy bear. I accused the man of coming on to me. I truly thought he had. He denied any such thing, and I was furious because I just knew without a doubt that something that he had said and the look on his face had caused me to have this thought. I wanted it to be true. Or maybe I was so humiliated I covered up with a furious look. He didn't back down for one minute, and I had to go about my business, feeling as if I had been attacked and made a fool of. Lots of shame there. Not the first time.

After the meeting in the loft with John, something felt clearer through me. I realized I couldn't "have" him—I had lived in neediness for fifty years related to Daddy's essential absence. The limbo of not being able to "have" my daddy was closing out—the chase was over. I felt free! The grieving surfaced from time to time, but at that point, I seemed to have moved into acceptance that this was the way it had been in my life and that this neediness had been at the heart of how I had related to men in my life for fifty years, projecting my stuff onto them. John helped me let go of much of my baggage about men. Time to settle deeper into my marriage with Ed.

The next day, I saw a Healing Touch practitioner for a session in her home. As sunlight streamed through her tall windows, she said, "All your chakras are open." She spoke about the *hara*—a term used in tai chi for the energy center near the navel—about how energy drops between the legs and goes up through the core star, between the pubis and solar plexus. "In your core star, I sense something having happened like the explosion of a cannonball. And that explosion caused a split or change in movement." She energetically initiated repair work. After that, she said that the *hara* was now straight, and that significant changes would be taking place because of this healing. The shift was affirmed.

During the healing, I lay quietly on her massage table, eyes closed, listening to gentle, flowing music. Colors passed before my closed eyes. I felt this healer's presence as she moved around me, holding a small vessel over me, lightly touching me—all my chakras, it turns out. Several times, the image of the figure of the Venus of Willendorf came to me within my abdomen. I had drawn her with colored pencils the previous night and experienced the strong sense of connecting with the goddess within. Thank you, goddess, for strengthening my power chakra—giving form to the good, loving, but not necessarily nice woman in me.

Chapter 46

RUTH

B y the time I was in my midfifties, I'd been sober eleven
years. One day, hearing that Ruth was in the hospital, I
decided to stop in and visit her. I hadn't seen Ruth since she and
her daughter Esther had attended Ed's and my wedding at Pixie's
in January 1996. I had been giddy with anticipation at seeing so
many friends and family gathered in one place, and how each had
dressed to the nines and was apparently happy with the union.
I had wondered if Ruth would come, and she did, dressed in
a blue brocade suit, wearing a gray wig. She came through the
door on Esther's arm and slowly walked into Pixie's living room
with a cane in her hand, heading straight for an elegant striped
silk bergère chair. For me this was the icing on the cake. Mom
and Crutcher and each of us six siblings greeted Ruth and paid
our respects. For a moment the family felt more complete. The
wedding photographer took pictures of us grouped around Ruth,
with Ed off to the side smiling benevolently over the scene.

While Ed waited in the car, reading *The Wall Street Journal*,
I found my way to Ruth's room. Esther, in her green nurse's aide

uniform, greeted me, smiling widely and pushing her glasses up on her broad nose. "Girl, I was wondering if someone from your family would ever get here to visit Mama."

I stepped into the dime-sized space Ruth shared with another patient on the other side of a thin curtain. Esther's hands glistened with the peach-smelling lotion she had rubbed into every crevice of her mother's eighty-five-year-old, cherry-brown body. I stood there not quite certain what to do, my neck muscles tensing at the shock of seeing Ruth so vulnerable and diminished. I had only seen her in full health before now. But Ruth looked content in her daughter's hands, and I remembered all the times she had rubbed my back.

"You like this, Mama?" Esther said. "I know you do."

"Hmm, hmm. Hmm, yeah," purred Ruth, eyes closed. She shifted slightly and reached for my hand. I had grown up alongside her stout strong body, her high thick waist, and breasts always caught in a brassiere and pointing straight in front of her. Now she had shrunk all over.

"I know you're there, Marilee," she whispered. "You and your sisters are my white daughters."

While I hugged Ruth, I glanced at Esther, who was about my age, and wondered how she felt about that. Esther didn't tease me the way her sister Cynthia had. Sitting in the presence of Esther, I felt a little uneasy and found myself wanting to pull out of the hug; the arms around me felt odd all of a sudden with Esther watching me hug her mother. I thought about my relationship with my mother. I realized that I'd never been able to "have" her either, that perhaps no one can really have her mother.

I was nervous about being with Ruth around her daughter Esther and covered it up by bringing up something I thought would be entertaining. "Ruth," I asked, "do you remember the day that Viola brought her cousin Fats Domino to the living room of our apartment on Walnut Street?" Viola ironed our clothes and sometimes babysat for us. She was darker skinned than Ruth and had a deep chortle when she wasn't sighing over the state of the world. Her steel-gray hair was fixed in a bun, and her eyes twinkled mischievously.

Esther's eyebrows shot up.

"Esther," I said, "you should have been there. The windows looking onto Audubon Park were wide open, and Fats pounded the keys and belted out *Blueberry Hill*. It was thrilling."

My arm caught on the room divider curtain as I waved it in an arc.

Ruth sighed, her face looking bemused, in spite of the fact that she was tired and sick.

"Then," I continued, "Mom returned home from her tennis game and shut us down. I think it was too much for her to have a black man in her living room if he wasn't working for her. You remember, Ruth? You were there watching all of the commotion. Remember how Mom said 'Viola, please thank your cousin and show him to the door.'"

Esther rolled her eyes and snorted. Ruth sighed again, maybe at Esther, maybe at the memory of my mother's action, maybe just because she was tired and catching her breath, or maybe she was wondering why I was talking about Viola and a famous black man and my own memories and mother while she was lying on her back, sick and tired. I grabbed onto that memory to cover up my embarrassment at being there with this mother and daughter, my shoulder muscles squinching even tighter near my neck. For a split second, I was aware of how loving touch was connecting this mother and daughter and how I had always longed for this, but had never felt accepted physically or loved for myself by my own busy mother.

I changed the subject again, this time to something I'd wanted to tell Ruth for years. "I remember when any of us felt sad, you always soothed us and helped us get to sleep. I'm so grateful you were there. What would we have done without you?"

"Always so much going on in your mother's house," Ruth said softly, compassion in her voice. I had felt secure when Ruth was there, even when our world swirled around in chaos. Her voice would go kind of singsong. I teared up hearing her now in the hospital.

By the time I was fourteen, Ruth had all six of us children to look after. She spent six days a week cooking and many nights babysitting while my parents attended Carnival balls, cocktail parties, dinner affairs, and tennis club soirees—sometimes it seemed like every night. Ruth put us to bed, listened to our stories, disciplined us with words, bathed us, fed us, fixed cookies and milk, but mostly offered her big, strong arms and warm heart.

During the day, Ruth tromped from our gray apartment kitchen through the Chinese-red bar pantry down the hall to brush Penny's hair or button Bruce's shirt or tie Allison's sash or rock baby John to sleep for his nap. She ran back and forth between the pots on the stove and our young selves, addressing our physical and emotional needs.

"Oh, honey, it's awright," she'd say as she stirred the red beans. "You can cry on my shoulder."

As with Pocky and Octavia, it had never occurred to me to inquire about Ruth's life beyond our walls. I never asked her who took care of her girls while she took care of us, even though I knew their dad was not in the picture. I never thought about how her girls might miss her, or how she might miss them or want to be home, hustling them off to bed, putting her feet up for a few minutes after a long day of caring for us. By day, she worked in a gray uniform preparing meals and smoothing over hurt feelings. She tried to tell us about her activities in so many words, but I couldn't hear them. There was no place in my experience to imagine she had a life, not just a social life but a life outside of my life.

Later, I learned that on her free nights, she'd chaired the Debutante Committee of the Original and Exclusive Twenties Social, Civic, and Pleasure Club—the same club that would host the ball Tom and I attended in 1981. For forty years, traditionally ten days before Mardi Gras, she zipped herself into a long white dress, pulled on white elbow-length gloves, donned a two-foot-tall glittery white headpiece, and ceremoniously introduced debutantes in her community to the families of their peers and club members. As she had always tried to do with us, she taught these young girls to become ladies—this aspect of Ruth stunned me and rocked my world—and she presented the debutantes at balls that lasted much longer into the night than the balls I knew. Tom and I had rudely left her celebration earlier than any other guests—it was embarrassing—so Tom could show up at his office the next morning.

I used to like the photograph that shows the two of us taken when I was Queen of Osiris, I in my fancy encrusted queen's dress with the big collar and Ruth in her uniform. But today I see in it reminders of class differences and the perpetuation of old power differentials. Instead, I now treasure another photograph of Ruth and me marking another milestone for me—Ruth and me dancing to the music of Papa Celestin's New Orleans Jazz Band at my wedding reception under the sheltering oak at Nain and E.O.'s Biloxi compound. She's wearing her starched dress-white uniform, apron, and low pumps, and she's penciled her eyebrows into two black arcs.

I remembered saying, "Come on, Ruth, dance with me."

In the picture, I'm standing next to her in my gorgeous white organza summer wedding dress with the long tulle veil— designed by me and made by the same artisans who had created my queen's dress. Ruth and I are laughing, champagne flutes in our hands. I can still feel the skin under my breasts perspiring from the July heat.

And Ruth socialized with the musicians and with members of Pocky and Octavia's family. I was stupefied as I watched her demeanor change to sweet and sexy around the band, a woman revealing never-ending surprises.

A few months after visiting Ruth in the hospital, one day at the end of September of 1998, Esther telephoned. "Mama wants you all to come by. She doesn't have much longer," she said. With a tone of acceptance, she said, "You are her white children, after all."

I picked up my sister Penny, and in the car on the way there, she was weepy. "I would have been a sorry chicken without Ruth's mothering," she said. "I claim her as my great protector and advocate. Mom was having babies one after another, and Ruth loved me through every step of the way."

Ruth had been an excellent role model, because Penny was a fierce and loving single mother to her two sons. I had no doubts that she felt comfortable with herself in large part because of the love and attention she had received as a baby from Ruth. Ruth was always good to me, but she adored the tiny baby born at the end of my parents' marriage, and Penny was her favorite of all of us. Maybe it was because of her sunny disposition and her vitality. Not that she didn't have her share of dark moments. Penny and I got along well—she was big-hearted and usually content in her own skin, and she bucked the system in her own ways. She didn't seem to have the tension and struggle I had about being myself in the midst of family expectations.

We parked in front of Ruth's house. It had been painted two bright shades of green since my last visit fifteen years earlier. The house stood halfway between St. Charles and Freret Streets in an area that had once been primarily white. One of my uncles had lived next door right before Ruth moved in. Single family and duplex buildings predominated, late nineteenth-century houses and shotguns situated alongside twentieth-century raised bungalows. I knew the neighborhood; it was around the corner from the original New Orleans Lawn Tennis Club, where I had spent hours hitting balls over the net and drinking Pepsi-Colas.

Esther greeted us from the front porch as we approached the front door. "It won't be too much longer." Esther was the daughter who organized Ruth's care. "She's had a long and full life. I suspect she's plumb tired by now. I know I am." We followed her inside and greeted Ruth's daughter Cynthia, who remained resting on the sofa. We met Ruth's handsome grandchildren and her deceased oldest daughter Bebe's children.

Cynthia said to Penny. "You were her favorite. She was always talking 'Penny this, Penny that.' Esther and I were her second-class daughters. You white girls got the best of our mama. But we love you." She smiled widely, with a hint of mischief and connection at the same time, looking just like her mother, gorgeous, broad, bright-brown sculpted cheekbones glistening.

"After all, we're sisters, one way or another. Go on in and see her." Cynthia pointed to the door into Ruth's dark-green bedroom.

I hugged Cynthia again and headed into the dark of Ruth's room to stand by her double bed.

"Ruth," I said. "It's Marilee. I'm here, Penny's here. I love you. I want to tell you how much I love you. You've given me so much of yourself." I smiled. "And you came to both of my weddings. I was so glad that Esther brought you to my wedding to Ed."

"Love you, too, Marilee. You're a good person." I could barely hear her voice. "Where's my Penny?" she whispered forcefully.

"I'll get her." I started toward the door. Penny walked over to the bed, knelt down, and leaned close to Ruth's head. Penny indisputably was Ruth's number one white daughter. I left them

together, choking on my tears, touched by this reunion, knowing that Ruth had loved me but that Penny was her favorite
and trying not to take it personally. On my way out the door, I
accidently brushed against an old chest of drawers, and turned,
taking notice of it for the first time. On top of the dresser sat
framed photographs of three or four generations of Ruth's family members, and a string of pearls hung on the mirror. Nearby
in a place of honor was a framed certificate for Licensed Practical Nurse with her name on it, reminding me that Ruth had a
whole other career after she stopped working for my family.

I reentered the living room with its high brick mantel painted
white. I took in the gold brocade sofa covered in protective plastic covering, the Zulu and other Mardi Gras mementos, a pair
of tribal masks, and more family snapshots. A large, framed,
tinted photograph of Ruth hung above the brick hearth. She
wore a blue suit with that same string of pearls as the one hanging on her mirror—her gray hair styled short and wavy. Such a
lady! Like my grandmother. Ruth worked for my mother, but
she had adored my grandmother, Nainnain, and talked about
what a queen she was and how she considered her to be a great
lady and role model.

I looked at the portrait and saw a resolute warrior and leader,
a woman who was astute, compassionate, kind, direct, and generous of self, with a boundless capacity for joy and leadership.

With so many people around, there wasn't time to tell her
everything I wanted to share with her. She was about to be
bathed, and then her supper would be brought in. She had her
own family to care for her. I felt disappointed and incomplete as
we left her house. I simply wanted to be among the family who
cared for her at the end, a remnant of thinking she was all ours.
The naiveté! It took me a few years before I wondered what it
would have been like to talk openly with her about race. We
never discussed these things in our life under my parents' roof.

It had never occurred to me at the time. So much affection and the intimacy of daily interactions exchanged, under protocols and pretenses never breached.

I learned at her funeral that Ruth lived her extraordinary life far beyond the walls of our house. I grew up taking her for granted, thinking her always present in the background of my life. "I have things to tend to," she would say. "I can't be sitting around here all day." How many ways did she try to show us who she really was? I saw only her role in our family until years later.

A few weeks after Ruth died, I had a vision come to me of an elephant, a large, gray, wrinkled elephant. I was participating in a workshop led by my breath work instructor. I breathed along with twelve others as I lay on my yoga mat bolstered by three pillows, enjoying the drumming that was part of the recorded music being played. I steadied my breathing and told myself it would be okay if I didn't go into the altered space I had read so much about.

I focused on the mix of music, bringing in African drums, rattles, and pipes. Slowly, after thirty minutes or so, I began heaving with sobs—drenching, deep sobs, and tears that streamed down my face. I didn't know what had hit me. I was regularly taking my meds, so I figured I wasn't manic. A vision of the elephant then came to me, big as life. Picture an elephant hovering over me on my mat. I sensed the presence of Ruth—it was the wrinkled skin. I thought about how much of our chaotic lives she had witnessed and how accessible she had made herself. She brought touch into our family—gave hugs, and spoke up for herself, which of course got her into trouble at times with my mother.

This didn't feel like the hallucinations I had experienced during manic periods. I chose to see this as Ruth's animal spirit coming to me, the spirit of the African elephant—powerful, social, matriarchal—reminding me of Ruth's wrinkled brown body when I had seen her with Esther in her hospital bed. Three days after this vision, I bought a small inexpensive pinky ring made of nickel at the Longue Vue Garden Shop. It depicted three little elephants—and I said to myself, *They stand for me, Pixie, and Penny, Ruth's white daughters.* Coincidental? It was too perfect, a soulful affirmation of the spirit visit. I bought the ring, wore it, rubbed it, and for a long time stared at it whenever I thought of Ruth's strong brown face and big embracing arms.

Chapter 17

THE SUIT

Everything about Ed's and my relationship seemed to go swimmingly, from our early days of dating and living together to our engagement to our wedding. Three weeks after my father died in 1995, Ed and I walked into Adler's Fine Jewelers on Canal Street and selected engagement and wedding rings. A modest inheritance from my father provided the peace of mind that helped me shift into wanting to remarry. That money, combined with my social work salary, allowed me some independence—which meant I didn't have to rely on Ed to pay my way, at least not entirely, and that felt exhilarating. Tom and I had had a very traditional marriage. Since then, I'd awakened quite a bit, so what had seemed fine financially with Tom didn't feel quite so fine with Ed. I couldn't foresee that I would soon realize that I truly was an independent woman—that I didn't have to rely on Ed for anything monetarily.

At our wedding two months later in January, I floated down the capacious wooden staircase at my sister's elegant high-ceilinged home on the arm of Trinity's first woman priest, one of the women with whom I regularly had supper on Friday nights. My untraditional blue Spanish lace dress symbolized to me that I was embarking on a new and different path. We processed through the wide hallway crowded with family and friends and into the living room in front of the fireplace where Ed stood. As he and I exchanged vows, I felt loving and bold and free. Yet at the same time, I harbored remnants of shame and worry about what other people thought about the twenty-one-year age gap between us. I felt so comfortable with him, and that overrode those other thoughts. I'm not sure how my father had felt about the age difference—he was only four years older than Ed. He'd never said anything when we were dating, and they'd seemed to get along well.

After the ceremony, Ed and I received our guests. Beloved Ruth was there in her brocade suit and gray wig. She hugged me tight and gave me her widest smile. When I spotted my mother, I received the first intimation that Mom and Crutcher might not be happy with my choice of a second husband. If they had given me hints earlier, I'd been too smitten to catch them. She looked elegant in her ivory white wool suit and pale jade-and-gold earrings, but I sensed little warmth coming from her. My parents' views still meant something to me, and I felt queasy when I saw the tight set of my mother's lips. *Oh shit*, I thought, *this is something more than about our age difference.* But I figured whatever it was would work itself out. I was mistaken.

During the weeks after the wedding, Ed came home to our Lakefront nest quiet and preoccupied. I finally got him to tell me what was bothering him. He'd been working on several projects in the Crutcher-Tufts office, but since 1992 he had primarily involved himself in putting together a potentially big deal in a Shell Oil field near Bakersfield, close to where Crutcher-Tufts already had another lease interest. Ed had flown out to the California field and told me he had come up with the idea that Crutcher-Tufts could do infill drilling, or adding new wells, in the fields where Shell already had wells, which could be highly profitable for Crutcher-Tufts. Ed knew the field intimately, ran numbers, calculated the potential tax consequences, and figured there would be a large sum of money involved for Crutcher-Tufts if Shell was in charge of operations and Crutcher-Tufts of financing.

In the fall of 1993, Crutcher's longtime business partner J. D. Tufts had died, and his attorney son, David, had taken over managing the firm. Crutcher fell ill that year, entered the hospital, and had stents put in. David then made major decisions for the firm, including changing the pattern of Ed's inclusion or participation on current and future deals. Crutcher unexpectedly, in Ed's opinion, aligned himself totally with his young partner, David. When Ed repeatedly put forth requests for what he considered as his fair share in the California oil infill deal, I understood that Crutcher and David backed away. For two years they held Ed at arm's length. Then, in 1997, Crutcher put David with his legal background into the negotiating position with Shell to work on the deal Ed had originated. Ed was all but shut out from participating in the negotiations and was denied his traditional share of the proceeds in a shift from the twenty-year pattern of working on deals together. Ed tried to talk with Crutcher, who pushed him away, and when Crutcher-Tufts, through David, came up with a new plan, it was unacceptable to Ed. He considered it unworthy of the effort he had put in and rejected it.

I felt heartbroken—crushed, really—that Ed and Crutcher were hardly speaking, and when they did speak about the deal, their respective perspectives were, in my mind, outrageously off-key, dissonant, on different wavelengths. What was Crutcher thinking? I wondered about David's role in the shift. It was as if he were whispering in Crutcher's ear that Ed had to go. Was he clearing the way for his own central role in the firm? The disagreement was not resolved through conversations. On March 13, 1998, two years after our wedding, Ed, frustrated and feeling he was not being heard, filed a suit against the firm before the statute of limitations ran out. This was not the way I had envisioned my new marriage would unfold.

What did I know? I'd heard Ed's story many times, and only twice had I spoken with Crutcher on the subject. The first time was over lunch at Cannon's Restaurant on St. Charles, wooden paneling at our backs, overlooking a patio with a banana tree in front of us where Crutcher at first had cajoled and teased me, trying to make me see it his way. I got defensive and emotional and raised my voice, causing a few heads to turn our way. Then Crutcher quit his teasing and stiffened into a brick wall. No dessert here. The second time, I'd called him and tried to bring up the subject, but he kept sidestepping, and we ended talking only about surface matters.

Later, when my mother and I met cautiously for coffee one afternoon, and I urged her to look at things differently, I saw lines etch into Mom's forehead and jaw—that hardening again. We finally agreed to meet for coffee from time to time—if I wouldn't bring up the subject of the disagreement. Looking back, I understand that my own viewpoint had congealed, and that meeting for coffee might be the only way either of us felt we could get together.

I'd dug in my heels, leaving little room for seeing anyone else's side of the suit. My loyalty to Ed was as much driven by stubbornness as the pigheadedness of those two old men.

It seemed to me to hold true for my siblings as well—not that I called and asked them; they didn't want to see other sides. In their minds, as far as I could tell, because of the complex way in which Crutcher had structured his business, Ed was not only suing Albert Crutcher and David Tufts and the firm; he was suing the whole family, including me, as a shareholder in various entities of the family business. I felt so defensive that I couldn't truly see that the whole family was being sued. I kept thinking, *This is about Crutcher and Ed.* Once I understood that suing the business indeed meant suing all of us, I had to return to my process. And I came to the same conclusion, even though Ed was suing me along with everyone else. I strongly felt that he had a case.

I don't know why I was so shocked at my family's reactions. We are an opinionated family, but I was so disappointed at the lack of nuance. Soon after Ed filed the suit, Penny and I had a talk sitting on the loveseat in my bedroom. Penny made it clear that she was furious about the suit. I immediately thought her objection might be because it threatened her security, but the moment when Penny turned on Ed—and on me—hurt the most. A couple of years later, Pixie and I had met on a bench on the edge of the Audubon Park labyrinth. At first, our conversation was all on the surface, but it quickly veered a little too close to the tender subject, at which point we said our goodbyes. I perceived Pixie as being protective of Crutcher, and although she was occasionally irritated by him, she was squarely in his camp, sometimes more than his blood children.

It seemed no one wanted to hear another side of the story. Not one person in the family said, "This is between Ed and Crutcher-Tufts—it's business" or "Ed must have a good reason for filing a suit." All I could say was that I thought Ed had a right to fight for what he thought he was due. And all they would say to me was "Against family?" Indignation characterized each side. The two legally involved parties had a first mediation in New Orleans—but it was a standoff. Neither side budged.

As the suit developed over the next few years, I became profoundly unhappy over the situation and pricklier than usual—especially when anyone said something pejorative about

Ed. Rarely happy with criticism, I fell into a cycle of defensive-ness about Ed's convictions and felt wounded by the rupture with family. I remained in denial that Ed was effectively suing all of us.

Three years into the suit, Christmas of 2001, the rift became painfully clear. Ed and I had been invited to Penny's for dessert. Everyone else in the family had been invited for the traditional family Christmas dinner, but we'd been invited for dessert only. All day, I'd felt a faint foreboding but had stuffed it down with the shame and hurt. I kept a lid on those feelings as Ed and I wove through Penny's living room, past the ten-foot blue spruce webbed in tiny white lights and ornaments, past relatives, mem-bers of the New Orleans white elite, among whom following a certain etiquette secures one's place in society—the fake gilded world I'd grown up in and still, now entering my sixties, fought to break free of. All around me were women in jewel-toned satin blouses, sweater sets, suits and skirts, shiny boots and high heels. Men wore polished loafers and colorful ties—red, laven-der, green, bright blue, silver. Some sipped bloody Marys, some virgin Marys, and most held a glass of Moet Chandon.

Where was Penny?

I nodded at siblings and cousins and spouses. Some greeted me, eyes lowered. Others ignored me and went on talking. I felt grateful that my uncle and his wife received us warmly as we snaked toward the open kitchen, the haze of people circling the center aisle, dinner plates in front of them or perched on chairs, plates balanced on their knees, forks clinking on china as they dipped into the green beans and mushrooms, savory roasted tur-key, and caramelized sweet potatoes. I'd been a fool to accept our invitation for dessert only, for thinking this small crumb meant everything would be all right, that we could put our dif-ferences behind us.

When we reached the kitchen, I saw Penny standing against

the counter and Mom, in her pepper tweed Chanel jacket and low Ferragamo heels, sitting in a chair at the back of the room, chatting animatedly with two of her granddaughters. My mother, holding court. *Surely Mom will take the high road*, I thought. *Surely, she will greet me civilly, appear gracious. For the family's sake.*

She locked eyes with me. I drew myself up and offered a smile. The muscles in her face froze, and her upper lip tightened in a thin line as she spotted Ed behind me. The veins in her neck pulled taut. My nieces stopped talking. *Was Mom gritting her teeth?* My stomach dropped. *Oh my God, she's refusing to say hello to me.* My heart fractured.

There was Penny in the kitchen. I caught her eye briefly as she observed the scene between Mom and me. My one ally in the family, Penny reached for her pack of cigarettes and turned away from us as she leaned back against the counter, as if to say, *I'm not jumping into that one.*

My shoulders drooped. I felt my body sway. Ed steadied me with his hand on my back. *Get a grip*, I told myself. How had I allowed myself to walk into this situation? I'd had every intention of putting on a good face—I had wanted to be part of family for so long. Now, cut off, isolated, I stood up and pulled my shoulders back. *This must be what's called facing the flak, Marilee. Breathe. Listen to your heart.* And my heart replied, *Look at yourself with love and get the hell out of here.*

I had insisted on dragging Ed into this morass even though I felt we wore second-class citizen labels—invited only for dessert. *How stupid was I? What had I been thinking?* I simply hadn't understood the extent of the bruising going on. And it hurt. Like hell. I felt a flush rising up through my shoulders and neck into the back part of my brain, expanding to my forehead and cheeks.

Trying to control myself, I focused on a photo of Penny as Queen of Atlanteans, one of the old exclusive balls of Mardi

Gras. It hung on the wall along with framed illustrated procla-
mations stating that she was Queen of Atlanteans and a maid
in Rex, the signature Carnival ball. New Orleans ex-Carnival
kings, queens, and maids often exhibited their royal upper echelon pedigrees this way and displayed crowns and scepters on
shelves and coffee tables. Mother still displayed the picture of
me as Queen of Osiris on her piano, despite how awkward our
relationship had grown. Saving face? During that time, I'd still
been a cog in the wheel of Uptown society, unable to differenti-
ate my thoughts from those of the group. I kept my own copy of
the photograph of myself as Queen of Osiris in a box of photos
at home. Maybe that picture of me, along with queen photos of
my sisters Penny and Allison, cemented my mother's place in
society, even though she had banished me.

Before we could leave, one of my nieces started serving dessert, and Mother circulated a word-of-mouth invitation to come
to her and my stepfather's house after Penny's, the house they'd
lived in since the 1957, where my three sisters, two brothers,
and I had grown up. The house where, traditionally, until this
year, 2001, my mother's side of the family had always celebrated
Christmas.

I walked over to my mother. "Are Ed and I invited?"

"Marilee," she said coolly, "you are welcome to come, but not
Ed." I looked her in the eye, turned around, and rejoined Ed,
who was talking to one of Penny's sons. He placed his hand on
the small of my back again; was he steadying himself or me? I
didn't know. We turned, I hugged my nephew goodbye, and we
left, without dessert, my heart pounding so loud it scared me.
Shame, my vicious companion since childhood, flowed through
every pore in my body as I reached for Ed's arm.

Thirty minutes later, Ed and I arrived at our home on Amethyst Street, a long way from where I'd grown up in the vicinity
around Audubon Park and St. Charles Avenue with its grand

and distinctive homes. We'd chosen this small home for its nearness to Lake Pontchartrain as well as its distance from the old neighborhoods. I loved our one-story, right-sized home, our heart place of comfort, relaxed and intimate.

Once inside, Ed drew me close and wrapped his arms around me. Shaking his head and nestling his forehead against mine, he said, "Your family is an enigma to me, beyond me." I let him hold me, comforted by his uncomplicatedness, this straightforward West Coast man who was puzzled by Southern conundrums and personalities and alarmed at my emotional reactions to family matters.

Ed went to take a nap, and I curled up on the red sailcloth sofa in the back room, warming my hands on my tea mug, savoring the heat seeping through, comforted by the familiar scent of peppermint. In the fading daylight, I looked through the glass doors that opened onto a backyard patio. My eyes rested on the forty-foot pine tree—catching the light from inside the house and from the back neighbor's outdoor lights—my touchstone to the forest. I stretched my legs out under the scratchy mohair plaid throw and took in the pleasure of being in such a comfortable room where we spent so much time, with its blend of Ed's books and my books on the cypress shelves, the mix of family pictures on the wooden trunk, the red-and-yellow Turkish rug, the warm, thick wooden counter of the open kitchen. This home had evolved from our combined pasts.

As I sipped my tea, my eyes wandered to a photograph on the bookshelf of one of my daughters, one of her two godmothers, and me. I thought of what her godmother had said to me when I'd told her about the legal battle. She'd looked at me hard and said, "Marilee, think about this. You have no idea what will happen if you support Ed. You'll lose your family." Those words rang in my ears now. It felt like death. A feeling of emptiness crept over me, and again I felt cast off, abandoned, kicked in the gut. It took me awhile to realize this rejection *was* a death.

I nursed my anxiety, struggling with the hurt, miffed at the whole entanglement. I was pissed at Ed for suing Crutcher, at Crutcher for discounting Ed, and a mite at myself for being so naïve. I had been taken to task by family members for not persuading him to give up the suit. When, after suffering the tortures of the damned, I'd eventually supported Ed's stance out loud, I'd found myself on the outs with my parents and my sibs. But I'd survived. I existed because of—and in spite of—this family I had let define me for decades.

This was a rare Christmas without the company of my mother's family, kicked out of the kingdom. And "kingdom" was an apt word. I thought of all the kings and queens in our family's past—all Mardi Gras royalty, of course. And I thought of my stepfather, a Texan who wasn't New Orleans Mardi Gras royalty but was still a man with dynastic desires.

Chapter 18

ℰxile

In spite of being exiled, I still believed that everything would go back to normal, that I could get my family back and stay married to Ed too.

The first hint that this was not going to happen came late in 2002, when Penny was diagnosed with a rare cancer that would claim her within a few months. During those months in 2003, I was slipping in and out of her home, driving Uptown from the Lakefront helping out, hovering, holding her feet, doing Reiki on her. A few days before she died, Penny invited Mom to climb into bed with her. Mom resisted at first, sitting primly in her chair, legs crossed, arms folded over her chest—and heart, I would say. But Penny wore Mom down, and she moved to the edge of her bed and let Penny hold her hand. Pretty soon Mom worked her way up next to her Penny, her head on her daughter's shoulder, and Penny brushed Mom's arm again and again. Mother and daughter. They looked blissful. I had to wipe away my tears and push aside a pang of envy at the rare closeness I was witnessing. I realized I was seeing exactly what I had longed for on this long journey from birth—physical cozy touch. There's no question in my mind that cancer-ridden Penny's luring Mom into her sickbed and spooning with her harkened back to Ruth's warm and loving touch she had experienced all her life.

But all was not well during those days Penny was dying. From her rattan daybed, leaning against three pillows and sipping a glass of shaved ice, pale yellow tint to her tanned skin, she implored me to persuade Ed to change his mind. I was so upset. She was the only one in the family I still felt true kinship with. She and I had a common language. And here she was challenging me.

While visiting Penny, I interacted pleasantly enough with other family members visiting on an almost daily basis. Things felt better, and I grew hopeful about my place in the family. After my Penny died on September 11, 2003, following her funeral, maybe it was my imagination, but I was no longer included in conversations. I felt dismissed, even by my sister Pixie. We'd both lost our beloved sister. We shared memories, losses, betrayals, and love. And it seemed she wanted nothing to do with me. I felt the same dismissal by other family members years later, in 2006, after my mother died. Was I being paranoid? Visiting Mom during the months of her last days with cancer, and spending hours in her bedroom with family members, I quickly became accustomed to seeing them again. But as soon as the funeral and the post-funeral family dinner ended, I felt the cold shoulder again from the extended family. That time I felt more pissed than hurt.

Over the years, I must have asked Ed to explain the situation to me a thousand and one times. I couldn't keep it straight. Maybe I couldn't take it all in—Ed was suing my family, and my family was fighting me, and Ed was also my family. A familial loyalty to Crutcher surfacing, I had initially opposed Ed's decision to sue and had looked for ways these two men—both important to me—could reconcile, as if I had that power and position. I admitted to confusion, wanting desperately for this to go away, wanting my family to like Ed, wishing everything to be okay. So naïve! My heart ripped, a raw, jagged tear down the middle. I felt angry at Ed for filing suit—it was my family, for God's sake—but simultaneously, I thought he was justified. It seemed to me that the firm had wronged him—I kept coming back to that—but I was unkind to him and yelled a good amount. This state of affairs was devouring our lives and happiness. I also felt shame sneaking into and around corners—the shame of being in such a position with so little control.

In 2003, around the time Penny was dying, I realized that although I really supported Ed, part of me still sat on the fence. The emotional strain had to give. By that time, a second mediation had taken place in Los Angeles—another standoff, leaving unbearable tension again.

One night that year, I had a dream about riding a whale. In the dream, I had a difficult time straddling this huge creature, and I realized that if I were to survive, I would have to shift and ride the whale sidesaddle. Riding sidesaddle signified for me a viable way to live. After all, my astrological sign is Cancer, and like the crab, I had sidled my way to my goals through life, with a hard shell that could change to soft. In my dream, it was clear that I would be in danger if I extended myself on both sides of the whale for too long—my pelvic structure wasn't strong enough for that. Outside the dream, I realized I would have to accept the fact that in spite of my pull toward family, and in spite of not knowing all the facts in the suit, I was aligned with Ed on this matter and was certainly not going to divorce him to show loyalty to my family, who couldn't entertain the thought that Ed might have a legitimate complaint.

I chose to ride sidesaddle to keep myself whole and intact, and I reined in a great deal of the energy it had taken to straddle both sides. I chose to honor myself, not so easy with my tendency to be pulled by this tension between family and wanting to live my own life. As I gained clarity and realized that divorce was neither necessary nor what I wanted, the gift of healthy separation from my family became plain. The cost of disentanglement was high. I missed them, but my grief was mixed with relief, and calm settled in. I was making my way toward feeling willing to break out of a rigid situation, and I could now say no—against family—this isn't right.

In the spring of 2004, a third mediation attempt was scheduled in Bakersfield. I planned to go for part of Ed's stay in Bakersfield to keep him company. I could drive out to the St. Philip the Apostle Catholic Church's labyrinth I had found by looking on the Labyrinth Locator website. I planned to walk the eleven-circuit labyrinth with its twists and turns and sit and meditate in its center. I had been walking labyrinths for five years and envisioned the St. Philip's labyrinth as a touchstone during the legal proceedings, a place where I could connect with myself in the god-forsaken city of Bakersfield.

A couple of days before heading to California, I talked with my labyrinth work partner and close friend, Margaret, about galvanizing support for myself in Bakersfield. Margaret and I had spent hours walking, planning, and facilitating labyrinths. "Why don't you ask Ed to find the labyrinth, go to it, and walk it for you?" she said. The labyrinth had helped me figure out how to think for myself, and it was just like me to think it would be the answer for another person.

I shared with Ed my desire to walk this labyrinth and asked him to go and check it out for me while he was in Bakersfield working before the mediation.

Surprisingly, he agreed to go.

A day later, I was seated at a table at a New Orleans restaurant with two of my Friday-night supper women friends, when

Ed called. In a surprisingly happy tone of voice, he said, "I'm beginning the walk out from the center now. I think I'll come back again. It's peaceful here." I visualized him standing in the center of the pattern, holding his cell phone up to his ear, and said, "I can't believe you're walking it! I'm so glad you found it for me, Ed." I looked up, eyeing my companions deep in conversation between bites of hummus and pita bread. I was very glad indeed, surprised, elated. When he said he wanted to walk the labyrinth again, I emitted a sigh and said, "Thank you," knowing full well he was doing this for me.

At a time of my deepest despair about the lawsuit, I said to myself, *Okay, the labyrinth can help me here.* I had observed myself riding sidesaddle on the great whale in my transformative dream, and I knew that I could allow that shift to be a mere adjustment that did not set me in opposition to the other side but placed me where love could suffuse each of our paths. Even as I chose to lead my life in marriage to Ed, I could choose to hold the situation, the players, and myself in my highest place of caring. I could love my sibs while leading my own authentic life. I was beginning to feel grounded more often, less like a confused child.

Walking the labyrinth helps me take sacred space for myself. When I walk it, I see that I can walk my own path while allowing others to walk their paths—definitely a handy tool when struggling with enmeshments. I did not have to choose either my husband or my family members—even if they continued wanting me to persuade Ed to "think right." I was not going to divorce this partner whom I loved and valued, who loved and trusted me, who was steady, intelligent—a determined and focused man, and the best feet-holder I know. I became more lucid about who I was, stripping away the illusions about—and unhealthy connections with—my family. I hoped to build a better, more genuine relationship with them, hoped that would still be possible. As I became more generous with myself, I began to get that I really was an independent woman. My concern about my age difference with Ed began to shift to a freer sense of worth. And my ability to support myself now gave me more of a sense of being an equal partner with him.

Two days later I received another call from Ed. "There's going to be a mediation meeting Friday."

"You're kidding!" I said. "So soon! Incredible! Ed, please settle if you can. This is so stressful."

Friday night his call came. "We're settling. I don't like all the conditions, but I'm ready."

I shrieked and said, "Thank you, thank you, and good for you!" After I hung up, I sat and wept from relief.

During this third and last mediation—after Ed's walk of the labyrinth in Bakersfield—the California judge ruled. I knew Ed wasn't getting anywhere near what he thought he was due, but I liked to think he had heard my plea to find an end to this mess.

My mind went straight back to Ed's labyrinth walk two days earlier. As soon as we hung up the phone, I'd called Margaret and told her the news. We high-fived over the phone and agreed that we would tease Ed: "It's the labyrinth." It just might have been that walk that turned the tide.

During the mediation, David Tufts must have assented to having a mediation check cut because I understood later that Crutcher had not. David wanted to get on with his own agenda—even though Crutcher refused to give him anything at all. I thought, well, what's done is done. I harbored the hope that my relationship with the others could now change. Little did I know.

When I spoke with my mother, her voice, anything but warm, came over the phone. "Marilee, you are so naïve."

I gripped the phone. Why did I always expect nurturing and acceptance from her? Why did I keep hoping, when deep down

I knew better? "The settlement doesn't change much," she said and hung up. Her comment pierced my heart. I put down the phone, hugged myself, and imagined that if I were a smoker, I would smoke right through a whole pack. Next thought, *Bring out the peanut butter!* and, thinking of Ruth who had often comforted me with a cup of peanut butter and jelly twirled together when I was a child hiding under the dining table, I asked myself if that was something I wanted to do. I gathered myself up and played some Margie Adam piano music to soothe my soul.

I came to realize that the real gift of these years of dispute was that I got to see who I was apart from my family of origin, whose motto could have been *lèse-majesté*.

At the same time, just as in the old story of an elephant that couldn't be seen completely by any of the blind men, I recognized that I was seeing only one part of the picture. The cost of this was huge. I could hear my siblings' voices: "Don't stay with Ed," "How can you betray Dad?" "Why are you doing this?" A crazy feeling that I'd betrayed family had plagued me for too long, even while I felt aligned with Ed. Was this survivor's guilt? I know that the disruptions and need to deal with these matters of Crutcher-Tufts business—and later, estates—must have taken up enormous energy, frustrating my siblings and others.

For us all to love one another as we lived our own separate lives, and for me to know that in some way our opinions added up to a whole—that might be as near as I could get. All I could do was pour love into and nourish my own heart, be grateful for the astounding gifts in my life, and hope to play with my siblings in the upper fields.

Chapter 19

CHANGING
OF THE GUARD

The year before Ed filed the suit, before the crisis hit and I was exiled, Ed and I attended the parades on Mardi Gras. My uncle, my mother's baby brother, was to reign as Rex, King of the Rex krewe, and I was eager to see him. He had sent us passes to ride in a limousine caravan to the Intercontinental Hotel to watch the parades and an invitation to attend the Rex Ball that night. I loved my uncle and wanted to honor him by participating in the day's parade and at the ball that night. I also anticipated the thrill of seeing my uncle reign as Rex following in my grandfather E.O.'s royal boots six decades later—the grandfather whose crown and scepter Lawrie, Pixie, Malcie, and I had discovered in his attic when I was nine. My anticipation of attending Mardi Gras again after five years away from Carnival formalities surprised me. A feeling of deep pleasure welled up in me, derived in embarrassingly large part from being closely associated with someone of status and importance and power and close to family. I felt a little confused by my behavior. And disheartened: it was the same old conflict between my love for family and tradition and my newly emerging path to be true to myself.

As we rode in the limo from the front of Tulane University across from Audubon Park through the crowd-filled streets down St. Charles, I laughed at myself and how excited I was. Once we passed Sacred Heart Academy on St. Charles, I craned my neck looking for familiar faces, hitting the jackpot several times when friends or acquaintances yelled at me. When I saw someone I knew near the limo, I shrieked and rolled down the window to connect. We drove past Ruth's Peniston Street neighborhood, past the Garden District where Tom and I had lived, and the Lower Garden District, past blocks of maskers reveling in Dalmatian spots, harlequin garb, and cowboy chaps and hats.

By ten o'clock we arrived at the hotel downtown, where open-air purple, gold, and green-festooned royal reviewing stands had been constructed for parade season, and huddled with the other invited guests, pulling our coats tight to ward against the cold. Ed and I found places on the bleachers just twenty feet away from the royal box, where I could see the profile of the smiling young Rex queen, one of that year's debs, dressed in a white wool suit trimmed in gold braid. She waved to the crowd below. The queen's kiosk was built on scaffolding covered with green awning cloth—not unlike the medieval stands from which kings and queens watched jousting. Her debutante court maids wore gem-colored wool suits with matching broad-brimmed hats that could have been made in the 1950s or 1960s. They were flanked by their mothers and Boston Club chaperones—wives of former kings and one-time queens—and nodded, chatted, and waved at the crowds in the street below them and across the way where the mayor and his entourage sat.

As Ed and I stood together on the Rex parade and peered

down the street for revelers and floats to pass by, my excitement grew. Traditionally, the floats of Zulu paraded early Mardi Gras morning, before the Rex floats. I could hear the sound of tambourines, drums, horns, and happy voices emerging from far down the street. The Tramp, a group of African-American laborers, came together in 1909 with one of their community's Benevolent Aid Societies, formed to provide financial help for members who became ill, and in 1915 started parading as the Zulu Social Aid and Pleasure Club. Its riders wore blackface, big wigs, and grass skirts to mock the elite white krewes, but for most of my life I had missed the mocking part. This morning, true to tradition, the Zulu krewe arrived first. Soon ten or twelve boisterous carousers appeared, marching and dancing between two Zulu parade floats. They twirled and stomped; I could feel the rhythm through the balls of my feet. Oh my God! There in this wild and merry dancing group I spotted my daughter Rebecca. She was in full Mardi Gras costume—hot pink, aqua, and white paisley satin pants, a bright pink shirt, iridescent pink wig, and pink puma sneakers—moving rhythmically to the lively sounds, basking in heart-driven joy, oblivious to the parade stands where I sat.

"Rebecca! Rebecca! *Bec!*" My heart in my throat, I yelled my head off in hopes she would look up and see me, ignoring open-mouthed looks from the folks next to me. I whooped at seeing her doing something I never had the nerve to do, and I envied her too. I cheered out loud that a daughter of mine could be so free. They passed by, without her having noticed me, but I was set up for the day, amused and delighted she was participating in this expressive way.

In the distance, behind the Zulu floats, the first Rex floats appeared. The king's float stopped in front of the royal box on our side of the street. My uncle, aka Rex, received toasts and gave toasts to his wife and the young queen high up in the royal box, and then turned to the other side of the street to exchange toasts with the mayor of New Orleans before rolling on to Canal Street.

Shivering there in the cold, I thought back to summer days in Biloxi when my uncle, thirteen years older than I, good-looking, fun-loving, and charming, had led us cousins in crabbing, softball, swimming, playing Dirty 8, and telling spooky stories narrated by his favorite made-up character, Jacobi. And how many times had he called me out to the dance floor at his various krewe balls? Such a charming and energetic dancer in his shiny mask, taking care of family.

Though the trappings of my heritage often caused me discomfort, I remained true to my upbringing in my own way, even though I had already begun to feel pushed out of my family and started distancing myself from that life. Yet something in me was still drawn to these social circles. The glamour, the familiarity, the shiny colors and costumes, the tribal rituals—the sense of belonging to the elite—all that held me. It was serious business for a circle of people who lived and breathed Mardi Gras much of the year. But whenever I went beyond brief forays into this world, I felt stifled by it and grew short of breath. I felt like closing my eyes and covering my ears to make it all go away.

Standing in the parade reviewing stand waiting for my royal uncle to arrive, listening to the noises, watching the action of the street, and smelling the beer, I remembered how one year, as a divorced single woman, I had attended the Krewe of Momus Ball and become impatient and humorless about the smell of sweat and alcohol emanating from the shiny sateen costumes and bodies of the masked dancers. I felt like an outsider in the midst of the picturesque rowdiness. So I had surrendered to an urge to get up and go, and rose from my seat between two other women in ball gowns, made my way to the end of the aisle, walked out of the auditorium, hailed a checker cab, and rode home. I felt empowered. I was discovering it was possible to leave that world, that I had a choice of how I wanted to participate in it, just as my daughters had seen.

At Carnival time the next year, in 1998, the year Ed filed the suit, I drove across Lake Pontchartrain north of New Orleans, away from the Carnival celebrations on my way to a weekend retreat for fourteen professionals. I parked and walked past a tall abstract sculpture into a spacious, high-ceilinged gathering room with wide pine floorboards heated by sunlight streaming through the generous windows that framed tree branches. Off to the right, deep colors attracted my eye, and I veered over to two tables and gasped at the richness of a crimson velvet gown trimmed in gold lying next to a black cape with silver trim. A whole table of goodies in the woods! What was in store for us? Social workers, energy workers, counselors, an art therapist, a naturopath, musicians, and yoga teachers would be my companions for the next forty-eight hours. It all looked auspicious, but I could feel the current of anxiety run through my body at being in a new situation.

After I had placed my considerable number of bags and totes in a corner, I greeted my breathwork teacher, one of the workshop leaders, and introduced myself to the other two.

By this time, Ed's conflict with Crutcher was causing me to redefine my relationship with family members—and with myself. I embraced going on the retreat—moving out of my comfort zone—hanging out with a new crowd that seemed to live reasonably with a disregard for elite krewes and balls. Losing myself in the breathwork and spending time with people whose values appealed to me nourished me splendidly. I looked around the meeting room and sent up a message of gratitude for the new circumstances. However, newbie on the block, I started out the weekend feeling uneasy and a little terrified, wanting to fit in, fearsome, really.

The potluck communal dishes each of us brought for the weekend inspired me. Observing others, I slowed down and relished each bite—quinoa, brown rice, adzuki beans, pinto beans, kale, endive, and radishes in a salad, kale, tofu, whole pecans, and almonds. I ate mindfully for a change—much chewing and munching. We ate that way for every meal, taking turns helping the leaders prep in the small kitchen.

On the first night, we sat on bleachers while one of the leaders who was a labyrinth facilitator described to us how Lauren Artress, an Episcopal priest at Grace Cathedral in San Francisco, had traveled with her vestry to Chartres Cathedral in France. Unable to find any cathedral clergy to grant permission, she'd removed the chairs that had been positioned on the eight-hundred-year-old labyrinth for the last two hundred years so they could walk this ancient pattern. She had then brought the pattern back to Grace and created Veriditas, the World-Wide Labyrinth Organization, and begun training people to facilitate and introduce labyrinth walks around the globe.

The Chartres labyrinth pattern next to the retreat house had been outlined in heliotrope paint on a twenty-five-foot asphalt basketball court, squeezed into half the space of the original forty-two-foot stone pattern. Our first night, blankets around our shoulders against the cool of the shadows, we lined up at the single opening to the labyrinth with instructions to go at our own pace. "There is no right or wrong way to move through a labyrinth. Follow the path to the six gracious petals in the center that are part of the center's design. Be open to whatever feeling, guidance, or understanding you might receive, and then, on your return walk, there's time to integrate your experience and carry it out into the world."

Because of the reduced size of the pattern, the walk was tight, and we brushed shoulders frequently, getting jammed up, some of us half dancing, playfully peering into each other's eyes, some in hermit mode, shawls over their heads. Respect and mindfulness took over and, amid some giggles and deep breathing, all was sorted out. Something about this pattern was distinct, and I had a liking for it, as if it were already imprinting on my cells. After the walk, I wandered slowly into the retreat center with the others, feeling peaceful and calm.

However, sleeping that first night—or I should say not sleeping—on a massage table was agony. I couldn't bring myself to stretch out on the floor! I used whatever mind control I could exert to keep myself still so I wouldn't fall off the table. I gathered my courage and effort to leave my chilled cocoon to go to the bathroom in socked feet and sweats. I felt self-conscious and terrified of waking others, embarrassed by the bulk of all that I had brought—bundles of bedding and blankets, clothes for whatever weather might come, journals, books. Gypsy, waif, orphan: take me in and make me feel safe; I wanted to go on a journey with the big folks.

When I got up early Saturday morning, since I couldn't sleep anyway, I piled on warm clothes and moved quietly out to the purple labyrinth. I walked it by myself to the sounds of a thousand roosters, birdsongs, and running water from a nearby stream below. I moved through the pattern and stood in holy moments there with my warm purple throw—Ed's first present to me—wrapped around my shoulders and over my head, transforming myself into a hermit figure. I was in rapture! What glorious moments they were, in cadence with the dawn noises on this ancient path. I floated my way back inside the communal building, counting the bushes on the way to ground myself, feeling an indescribably deeper connection to myself.

By Saturday afternoon, ease had set in. The leaders' ease allowed me to connect with them readily, and through them, with the others. I felt enough a part of the group to relax, enjoy myself, and join in the exercises with costumes—I donned the red velvet dress and later the hermit cape. After meditating, I drew two mandalas that confirmed for me my desire to be in the outdoors—tears, trees, greens, sun, a woman in goddess stance with her arms and hands reaching joyfully to the sky. Then I chose to sleep in the dormitory for the second night with people using sleeping bags instead of tossing and turning on the massage bed by myself. I instructed myself to show up, that I'd catch up on sleep later if I couldn't sleep for the second night in a row.

I appreciated being with new guides and discerning creative ways to be alive. To have started the Mardi Gras season this way signaled to my inner self a turning point, a new way of being and spending time. My early fears had become part of the journey, and my fright turned into delight. I loved the barely lighted trees in the woods outside the windows, the wooded walkway down to a river. By the end of the forty-eight hours, a feeling of harmony flowed in me and gave me a taste of what I yearned for—a deeper connection with myself and with the planet. This retreat resulted in refreshment.

Lady Bountiful, Goddess of the Edge of the Forest as well as the Beaches, thank you for the opening of doors I've yearned to go through and for which I have been preparing myself.

A few years later, one of my last years living in New Orleans, I spent Mardi Gras pruning in my garden behind the house where Ed and I lived. The elderberry tree looked a little bare, but I knew it would be healthier in time without all those straggly branches. I trimmed a few more dead branches from the cigar plant and nicked my palm while weeding the potted lemongrass. I stood up and walked around the circular bed, peering into some Spanish lavender that wasn't exactly thriving—too wet and too hot here. It needed to go. Impatiens would probably take over anyway. I slowly crossed the thick St. Augustine grass in my bare feet, avoiding sharp-edged cones, over to the tall pine tree in the corner of the yard, touchstone for woods I loved and didn't yet know. I leaned forward and embraced the tree and thanked it for being there. I was aware that the pruning of my plants was a mirror for what was happening in my life. As I turned back to the patio and the house, I reminded myself that I could still watch some of the Rex and Comus festivities on TV that evening. I laughed to myself, one minute ecstatic in the backyard, the next focusing on the festivities on TV. I have many aspects to myself.

Whether I went to the Mardi Gras or stayed home and tended my garden, my ritual during my last years in New Orleans included tuning in to Errol and Peggy Scott Laborde's televised *Meeting of the Two Courts of Comus and Rex*. Sometimes I would fall asleep watching Rex and the Comus Queen promenading around the floor and the monarch Comus escorting the Rex Queen around in their joint Grand March, but I had to watch—it was just part of what I did.

I often caught sight of couples dancing and the shiny magenta and rich citrine velvets, the beautiful azure-and-gold silks of the ball gowns, the Marine band that always played so precisely. I was still vulnerable to the lure of the familiar rituals and the thrill of seeing people I knew transformed into storybook figures on television. I often watched way past the time that it was interesting to me, like eating a few too many chocolates from a gift box long after you're full. Enough is enough.

Chapter 20

HANDS ON, HANDS OFF

A s I continued exploring the world beyond Mardi Gras, kings and queens, Garden Club, and Junior League, I found myself doing things I never could have imagined doing before. I was learning to be myself, choose for myself, sing out loud. One afternoon I found myself driving to a weekend Reiki class. I had heard that a Reiki treatment balances the body so it can heal itself if ill or in pain or in need of being refreshed. It affects the vibrational body, and the practitioner is empowered by her Reiki Master with the ability to access it with symbols and ceremonies. I had liked the people I met who practiced Reiki healing, and I longed for the peace, calm, and fun they seemed to have. I'd told Ed where I was going—I wasn't one for keeping things from him—despite my initial apprehension that he would think it sounded outlandish. But as I drove down a pine-shaded street near the Mississippi River levee looking for a parking place, words of self-doubt and recrimination ran through my mind. *You can turn this car around and go home now. You're nuts to be doing this. Who would ever believe it?*

When I parked my car in front of the host's home, I took a deep breath. I felt pulled to step into this new arena. I really wasn't sure what Reiki was, but I was inexplicably drawn to it and liked what I'd observed in the company of a few people who were into it. And I was aware that taking an exploratory step like this, even though others may not understand, bolstered my sense of being my own person.

The host, Elizabeth Pellegrin, greeted me at the door with a hug and invited me into her home. After visiting for a few minutes, I found a comfortable spot in her living room, where an ocean-blue Reiki table, similar to a massage table, dominated one end of the pine-paneled space. Others trickled in, including a beautician, massage therapist, psychotherapist, filmmaker, university professor, and two ten-year-old girls who arrived with their mothers.

Elizabeth introduced a swan-necked woman as our teacher, a Reiki Master from Canada who wore a hip-length, peacock-blue embroidered jacket. She asked each of us to say why we'd come. *Oh no, I didn't come to say anything. This is not what I bargained for.* When my turn came, I said I liked what I'd seen in other Reiki practitioners—a sense of calm and a radiance that came from inside. I didn't add anything about my simultaneous urge to be there that was at odds with risking my status quo.

"The first thing to learn as a practitioner is to treat yourself." Our teacher placed her hands over her eyes and forehead. Then she demonstrated several more positions. By this time I was questioning the wisdom of even being there. I felt a little spooked. Imagine a room filled with people placing hands on their heads, moving their hands silently down their clothed bodies at five-minute intervals, hands on, hands off. I kept peeking at my neighbors to see if I was doing it right.

After an hour she said, "Now we'll start the first of three initiations you'll receive this weekend," and disappeared into the bedroom. Two at a time, we filed into the room, which held a pair of chairs, a chest with photographs of lineage bearers, and a refreshing vase of daisies and tulips. When it was my turn to be initiated, I didn't feel anything special except the strength of energy focus in the teacher's initiation. The whole class regrouped in the living room, and we spent the rest of the weekend learning hand positions for treating another person. Then we spent hours practicing. After that, the group split up for the evening, and I drove home.

The first thing I did at home was to recruit Ed for a practice treatment. "Ed, please climb up on the kitchen island so I can treat you."

"What? Climb onto the island?" He sounded a little incredulous and poked fun at the idea, but finally indulged me.

I tucked an armload of pillows and cushions under and around him to make him as comfortable as possible on the hard surface. After I completed treating him, I asked, "How was it?"

He looked at me sleepily and said, "Nice, but it didn't do anything for me."

I returned to a full day of Reiki and finished the workshop the next day with a commitment to treat myself every day. I began rising early in the morning to treat myself. It was hard for me to stay still and hold each position for five minutes—I was jumpy and impatient. I saw my new Reiki pals at weekly Reiki exchanges and continued treating myself daily.

A year later, my teacher returned to New Orleans, and I took her Level II class with six other students, practicing what we had learned in Level I, and then adding the two Level II symbols. This group seemed deeper into Reiki than I felt I was, but eventually, tracing the symbols in my mind became natural and part of my daily practice. I loved the inner space it afforded, and usually emerged centered and refreshed with a deepening sense of inner calm and guidance. I wanted to do Reiki on everyone close to me in the beginning—to share the wealth and healing—but slowly learned I could be overbearing about it. I have treated myself with Reiki, to help with situations in my family, relationships, and people requesting help, but I try to be mindful and no longer expect others to like what I like.

A couple of years later, on a summer evening in the early 2000s, I hosted Elizabeth's Reiki Circle at the house I shared with Ed. That evening just before the guests arrived, Ed supported me by good-naturedly retiring with his book to our bedroom sofa. I felt jangly, unsettled, but I told myself to breathe in and exhale. I really wanted to have this Reiki energy in my home. I knew from past experience that by the end of my treatment, the jangles would pass. After doing a few downward dog yoga postures next to the Reiki table, I felt better. Then my Reiki pals arrived to set up for our Reiki exchange. One person would be the recipient of Reiki through the hands of everyone else around the table, and then that person would join others as a new person climbed onto the table to receive a treatment. Then a new person would rotate in, and another, until everyone had received a treatment.

Elizabeth opened my Reiki table and flipped it upright. The light outdoors was fainter now.

I went first, lying on my back, comfortable with a small rolled towel under my neck and a pillow under my knees. I asked for a light cover to pull up over my body, and then one person stood at my head and two others on either side of the table. I felt their hands rest lightly on my body. My head, feet, and torso were held by the others with tenderness and respect, and I moved into a sense of timelessness, the light blanket adding one more layer to my cocoon. It was delicious. An embracing and safe peace—an unfamiliar bliss—lifted me into a place of oneness with my surroundings. As I was flying with the angels, I felt boundless space with no fetters, my heart breaking wide open—freedom.

During another treatment, at another exchange of Reiki at my house, I spent most of my time on the table in grief, releasing sorrow that had been locked up in my body for a long time. This time, as I had before, I felt held by the practitioners and grateful for the clearing, grateful for feeling joy that was different from mania. When they were finished, I sat on the edge of the table and drank a full glass of water as I consciously came back to the room. Then it was my turn to give Reiki with the others.

Later, when Ed and I decided to move to Seattle, I signed up for the four-day Northwest Reiki Gathering in August at Breitenbush Hot Springs west of the Willamette Forest in Oregon. Before Ed and I left town, I went to Elizabeth's initiation as Reiki Master in her home. A dozen of us squeezed into a small sacred room. I experienced solemnity and joy in witnessing this act of commitment. She had waited thirteen years before she chose to be initiated. I saw that whether it took thirteen years or three, becoming a Reiki Master was a serious matter not to be taken lightly or precipitously. I would keep that in mind over the next few years. I googled Reiki Masters in Seattle, and once Ed and I were settled in our new apartment, I joined Gretchen Munsey's Reiki Circle. In August, I drove with her and Arlene Angell, another circle member, to Breitenbush.

Because I'd signed up late, the only accommodation available for the first two nights was to stay solo in a tent. After that, I'd have room in the lodge for two nights. *What the heck? This is a year of adventure*, I thought. I had camped only once, so cloistered a life I'd led! A true Southern flower. That night, after dinner and a visit to the library in the lodge, Arlene and Gretchen, along with the eighty or so other Breitenbush guests, went off to their cabins while I headed for my tent, flashlight in hand, evening light barely visible.

I made my way down the path through a wooded area, feeling lost, on uncertain ground. *Plug on, Marilee!* The light was faint now, the shadow of the mountain giving off a lavender glow. I felt the temperature drop within minutes; the warm afternoon had gotten markedly cooler. I inhaled the sharp scent of pine and fir in the forest around me. *Delicious! Maybe my tent will be nice and cool.* I had borrowed Anne Phyfe's sleeping bag, and my duffel bag bulged with one blanket and three sweaters. I congratulated myself on being so adventurous. Not easy for an ex-queen with curtseying and scepter-waving skills who enjoyed being waited on. *Oh wonder!* What would my life look like if I had learned outdoor skills rather than queenly ones?

The temperature had dropped to the low fifties from the high eighties of the afternoon. I could hardly unbutton my shirt. *Shit, it's cold!* Why hadn't it occurred to me to ask about the weather in the summer? My tight neck and shoulder muscles contracted even more than usual. I felt three inches shorter. The mountain air hit the back of my neck. *Brrr!* I had not for one moment anticipated this cold. I had trouble pulling on my pajamas, and then I lay in my bag, piling everything I could on top of me, including all the sweaters I had brought and my fleece vest. The tremor in my hands wouldn't stop. And worse, I couldn't get the zipper on the sleeping bag to work. I lay there, my whole body shivering with nerves and cold and regret for my incompetence.

I tried to will myself to sleep. If only I could get the zipper fixed. *Oh hell, where's the damn flashlight?* I gave up trying to fix the zipper and lay awake, shivering, fighting a migraine, dehydrated but afraid to drink water lest I'd have to go to the bathroom. I tried to roll onto my side and felt something hard— the flashlight. *Thank heaven.* I reminded myself to breathe. I missed Ed. I missed our warm and comfortable bed and snuggling up against his body.

Still awake at three a.m., I made myself pick up my flashlight and go to the shower house to pee. I stayed there ten minutes, grateful for the relative warmth blasting from a radiator. When I headed back toward tentville, I stopped in my tracks, caught by the utter stillness, the rustling of the trees, the quiet. I looked up, stunned at the sight of the white mass of stars through the tall trees. I couldn't take my eyes off the brilliance of the sky. Had I ever seen a night sky like this with this clarity and crispness of the stars? Stillness. Awe. I stared up at the starry sky between the treetops, listening to the rush of the river, breathing in the scent of the forest. This sacred place, these ancient trees—pure, clean, and holy air.

And then, in the midst of the quiet, a thought came to me: *Reiki the zipper.* Ha! I made my way back to the tent with renewed vigor, wriggled into the sleeping bag, placed my Reiki hands over the jammed zipper for, what—three, five, ten minutes? I maneuvered the two parts of the zipper, releasing it, *rearranged myself, then re-zipped the sleeping bag. Triumph! A four o'clock in the morning miracle! End of unsought vision quest. The prospect of sleep!*

The second night, warmed by Breitenbush hot spring pools and friendly conversation, I felt calmer. I thought of people around the globe who had grown up with this access to the skies and to ancient sacred lands. I felt ecstatic taking fledgling steps in such a large northwest community focused on things fascinating to me. Three months earlier, I'd said goodbye to family and friends in New Orleans, and here I was, on my own, in the middle of nowhere, healing zippers. I am blessed. I am blessed. I am blessed.

Chapter 24

GO NOW

In 2004, after the suit was settled, Ed and I talked more frequently about changing locales.

In the early 2000s, the thought that I could actually live in the Pacific Northwest seemed ludicrous. I had harbored periodic urges to go west since my visit in 1965 with the Websters in San Francisco and Mendocino, and my urge had grown stronger. I still grated over the fact that I hadn't been able to go to Berkeley on a fellowship. Ed had grown up in California and had indicated partiality for the West Coast as well. He had grown up in the central and more northern part of the state—Modesto, San Jose and environs, Petaluma—and loved to talk about fishing trips with his father along the Klamath and other rivers when the salmon jumped in packed streams, and about taking in too much sun on the Carmel beaches.

After several visits to Seattle to see Anne Phyfe as well as Ed's older son, Regan, who lived nearby with his young family, we were leaning toward adopting Seattle as our new home. I liked Anne Phyfe's husband, Bez Palmer, wanted to dote on my five-year-old granddaughter, Lily, and longed to take classes in Anne Phyfe's burgeoning yoga centers. The appeal of Seattle's distinctive neighborhoods also attracted us. Seattle's trees and parks, contours and backdrops of snow-covered mountains, and proximity to the waters of both the Puget Sound and Lake Washington resonated with my idea of a heavenly place. And I was already imagining that Anne Phyfe's studio would provide me with much solace as well a place to practice yoga. To look out from a ridge and view sea and mountains—particularly massive Mount Rainier with its sun-tinted snowy facets—lured me, not to mention the pull of an entirely different culture.

Then, in early 2005, I read *Rising Tide* by John M. Barry, a book about the disastrous 1927 flooding of the Mississippi, and Mike Tidwell's *Bayou Farewell: The Rich Life and Tragic Death of Louisiana's Cajun Coast.* For the first time, I became aware of and began paying attention to what could happen to the Louisiana coastline in the event of a catastrophic hurricane. I saw clearly that the barrier islands were disappearing, and because of that, our city stood vulnerable to heavy flooding. Maybe leaving was a good bet.

Even as I was looking toward the West Coast, I had many ties to my beloved, complicated New Orleans. After all, Jennifer was settled across the river in Algiers with her husband, Chris, and the Arnone clan, and Rebecca was finishing up her documentary. I was connected to my small Reiki community and had aligned myself with people interested in walking and building labyrinths and with Judith Linden's group. I'd joined three other women to form the Friends of the Labyrinth at Audubon Park, which had helped orchestrate a huge effort to build a permanent labyrinth in the park that would be accessible to the public 24/7, a welcome shift to the secular from my work with labyrinth in the church. I would be leaving behind these groups as well as four or five friends I had known through the decades, but most important were my two daughters. The thought of physically moving frightened me.

Ed and I rented an apartment in Seattle in June 2005 to see if we liked living there before buying a house. Within three months, we had decided to stay in Seattle. Our decision at that time—just before Katrina hit—was the end of a long and complex but serendipitous journey.

During the period from late 1990s into the early 2000s, after my 1998 retirement from social work, I discovered through friends a local source of heart-based nurturing at Dr. Antoine Ky's Chiropractic Clinic on Canal Street across from the streetcar barn. A fifth-generation healer, Dr. Ky had abandoned medical training in New York and Paris to pursue the healing work he had learned growing up in Vietnam and later in Paris. He, along with his radiant staff, was passionate, loving, and kind. Whenever I crossed the threshold into Dr. Ky's harmonious space, the ground floor of a raised cottage on Canal Street, I felt a sweet, healing, positive, and sacred energy.

One weekend, I traveled with Linda Moore—an adorable, petite, red-haired angel and friend on Dr. Ky's staff—and Dr. Ky's oldest daughter to Mississippi for a weekend-long medical intuitive training. His daughter was a serious student and planned to follow in her father's footsteps. Linda had been offering energy sessions in her home for many years. I felt a little out of my league, but I had gleaned a few things. During a session on reading auras, no one had any trouble seeing them. I told myself I would try but would take it in stride if I didn't see anything. I followed the instructions. As a woman stood in front of a white cloth hung on the wall, I lined up with other workshop guests for a turn at reading her aura. Some people could see layers and layers of aura—different colors. One person could see nothing. When it was my turn, I miraculously pushed all other thoughts aside and concentrated with my eyes and brain on seeing what I could see. I surprised myself when I saw a bit of a yellow aura, enough to believe that it could be done, and I knew that if I wanted to concentrate on seeing auras, I could become proficient. In the meantime, it was a delight to spend time with Linda and Dr. Ky's daughter and to be around their light energy.

On September 11, 2004—a year to the day after Penny died—I was in Dr. Ky's clinic and was getting up from the treatment table where Dr. Ky had been working on my left neck and shoulder area, when Linda Moore walked by and called my name.

"Wait, Marilee, are you free right now? Would you like to see Ron Hall? His scheduled client just called to cancel."

"Who is he?" I asked.

She looked surprised—as if I should know who he was—but answered, "He's a healer with real psychic gifts. Dr. Ky admires him greatly, and when he comes to town from Georgia two or three times a year, he rents space upstairs for his sessions. I can't believe I've never mentioned him to you. Everyone sees Ron when he comes to town." She sighed, half-smiled, and gave me an apologetic hug.

Healers, fine. Psychic gifts I wasn't quite sure about. I never would have considered seeing a healer like this if I hadn't already met and listened to Judith during biweekly gatherings in the late 1990s. I had begun a process of learning to trust myself and to stop worrying that anything I did that was out of the ordinary New Orleans world—or even Ed's or my daughters' or my friends' worlds—meant I was crazy. With Judith I had learned to silence the voices that held me back—*You can't do this. What will others say? How will it look? You'll fall into a black hole. You'll be the crazy you've tried not to be for ten years*—and trust my own voice inside. At Judith's gatherings, I heard new, merciful phrases that helped me accept myself, without my family's or other external approval: *Know that you are loved. You are love. Learn to be supported by the universe. Tell your consciousness you are complete. Say, "Does this thought or action lead me away from the light?"* Over the years I'd had a few individual readings from Judith, too, and had always gleaned new perspectives and ways of seeing things from them. Working with her had paved the way for me to try Reiki, and now it was paving the way for me to see this healer with psychic gifts recommended by Dr. Ky.

I didn't take her or Dr. Ky's recommendations lightly. And I thought seeing this healer might be a good way to celebrate the anniversary of Penny's passing. The girls would be in school until three, so I had plenty of time to meet with Ron Hall, if it seemed right to me.

When I met Ron in the well-lit, wide central hall above Dr. Ky's clinic, he invited me to sit down on a yellow-cotton-slip-covered sofa. As I sat, he lowered himself into the single chair to my right. I guessed he was about fifty, and I had the sense that I had known him forever. After our initial hellos, he asked me a few questions. Then he told me a little about himself, primarily that there had never been a time when he hadn't felt "presence." His family had been supportive of his gifts from the earliest age, so he had never had to suppress or hide them. He said his work included seeing individual clients and offering energy trainings—weeklong sessions teaching his "awakening" work.

After we talked some more, he handed me several crayons and a few sheets of paper. He told me to draw and said that my drawing would aid him in his discernment about me. I willingly took up the crayons, closed my eyes for a minute, and began drawing whatever came to mind—a mountain, raindrops, human figures. After about ten minutes, we resumed talking, mostly about my complex family relationships, the lawsuit, Ed, and my daughters. Ron said something lovely and on target about each of my daughters, as if he knew them. I was fascinated. He then said the session would eliminate energy blockages and effect past and present healing.

"Let's walk across the hall into my treatment space," he said, getting up from his chair.

I climbed up on the massage table in the middle of the tall-ceilinged room. Ron explained that a team of surgeons would come in if needed to do "psychic surgery", and that one in particular was in charge. I had heard of psychic surgery—I had read of the work of John of God—so I went with it, curious but silent. In at least one case I had heard of, the psychic surgeon gave over his consciousness and incorporated the spirits of past doctors and saints. These entities gave talks, examined the waiting masses, and conducted the visible and invisible operations. I wondered what would happen here.

I remained conscious most of the time, forty-five minutes or so, but barely at some points. I heard the intermittent clang from a Canal Street streetcar and smelled the candle burning. I heard Ron breathing, talking to himself, and talking to his guides. I felt totally relaxed.

When Ron was done, he touched my shoulder and said, "Ground yourself before you get up. Take your time. No need for surgeons," he said, "but a lot of healing took place." I felt energy run up my back, a sense that what he said was true. I felt seen, recognized, and buoyed by this experience, but I didn't think it was life changing.

I wrote out a check for him, said goodbye, and left.

Four months later, Linda called to tell me Ron was returning to New Orleans in January 2005. I made my second appointment with him. This time, the effects of my research about the river, flooding, and disappearance of coastal lands fueled questions I had for him. I told him that Ed and I had been toying with the idea of moving to Seattle or somewhere in the northwest. I wanted to know if he had any guidance concerning this.

After a few seconds he said, "My guidance tells me that Seattle is one of the areas okay to go to." He paused and sat on the edge of his seat, leaning forward and looking me straight in the eye. "Go now," he said. "There may be a catastrophe there sometime, but it won't be devastating. You will be helping other people when it's needed. I see you there, one of the people helping others to find healing, wearing white, walking the streets of the city touching people on their foreheads. Pick up and go now. Go before the fall. *Go now!*"

He was so definite. I felt I might be crazy to be listening to him. Could I really leave Rebecca and Jennifer, my friends, and our adorable and comfortable house on Amethyst Street where Ed and I were so happy? How could I tell people that I was moving to Seattle because a man named Ron had said, "Go now"?

As wild and haunting as this command was, it aligned with my spine. And when I mentioned it to Ed, he did not challenge me.

By mid-March, Ed and I were driving around Seattle, exploring, poking into different neighborhoods, trying to imagine living there—and liking the idea. On the last day of our trip, we put down a deposit for an apartment that we could move into on June first.

Sometime early that spring I told my three daughters that we were moving, in large part because we were concerned about the geography of New Orleans, about the shrinking barrier islands that had always played the role of protecting our city. But we all knew there were so many other reasons, including a desire to comfort Anne Phyfe and Bez on a heartbreaking recent loss of their son, whom Anne Phyfe had carried for five months, and of course, the aftermath of the suit. It felt good to be putting geographical distance between me and the family that I felt was still cold-shouldering me.

When I returned to New Orleans from that March trip to Seattle, I signed up for a weeklong Awakening training with Ron Hall in Georgia. I thought it would be perfect before I left for a new home in a new city. It was a huge stretch for me, but I felt a pull to do it. I wanted to learn more about energy work.

One Tuesday morning in April, I was packing to leave for Ron's workshop when one of his longtime students called me.

"I'm sorry to be the one with this news for you. Ron Hall died this morning. I'm so sorry."

I held the phone away from me in disbelief. "What?" I said, finally.

"This seems unbelievable, I know," the woman said. "I am so sorry to give you this news. It's so sudden."

"That is awful, just awful. I feel as if the wind has been knocked out of me. I can't believe it. I'm sure you can't either."

"I am so sorry you won't get to study with him. Such a wonderful being."

As Ed and I drove into Seattle on June 1, 2005, heading for our new apartment on Capitol Hill, I thought, *Goodbye, Louisiana; goodbye, kings and queens. I am taking a break from you. Hello, Seattle and the Northwest and your forests and mountains and island and large Reiki community.* I felt excitement—and wondered when the grief would come, when I would allow myself to feel it.

Chapter 22

ⅅ̃ISASTER ℤONE

E d and I moved into a postage-stamp-size Seattle apartment a half mile from Anne Phyfe and Bez's house. When they came to visit, their daughter, five-year-old Lily, my first grand-child, would burst forth from the elevator door on the fourth floor before spending the night. An entire wall of our ten-by-twelve living room was covered by a four-by-five-foot painting of two terns flying high in the night sky, drawing into a moon painted from hundreds of disciplined blue doodles. I had fallen for this cosmic work by Mexican artist Alfredo Arrequin shortly after we moved to Seattle. When she stayed over, Lily and I slept on a queen-size air mattress under the painted terns and the stars and moon. During this honeymoon time in Seattle in 2005, Ed and I explored different distinct neighborhoods, thinking about buying a house, punctuated by visits to nearby Madison Park and Madrona beaches, where Lily and her friends played in the cold Lake Washington water.

In mid-August, I took off for the Reiki gathering in Breit-enbush, Oregon. I had been back in Seattle from the gathering about ten days, getting into a routine of accompanying Anne Phyfe and Lily to the beach, visiting coffee houses with Ed, and taking yoga classes at the yoga studios owned by my daughter, when I heard that a powerful hurricane was bearing down on New Orleans. I felt a chill run up my spine and wondered about Rebecca and Jennifer and their situations. There was no way to reach them by phone. Landline and incoming cell phone service were both knocked out at that point.

Ed and I spent days fidgeting in front of the television, following the storm, the breach, the mishaps, and the stranded and starving people waving for help from attic windows. And I wept.

The devastating breach of one of the protective canal levees altered life in New Orleans as we knew it—eight blocks from our Lakefront neighborhood house. This breach and two others farther east left much of the city underwater for days with the unforgettable results we all watched on TV. I went on the Internet and determined that our house that stood a block from the lake levee was amazingly on high enough ground to remain dry after the breach. I could actually see the bird's-eye-green L-shaped backyard. The area beyond, as much as two or three miles of it, was completely devastated by floodwaters.

Back in New Orleans two months later, only five months after our move to Seattle, the full nightmare of Katrina forced itself into focus. Here was reality. As Ed and I crossed the 17th Street Canal overpass, a brilliant blue sky crackled, incongruent with this stretch of brown-gray earth. A wasteland of waterlogged houses, fallen wires, and trees spread around me, everything dulled by layers of dried silt and sludge. The small-screen images of the aftermath of Katrina I had watched on TV were scant preparation for this violent homecoming. This was only seven weeks after the August 29, 2005 storm, and we had flown from Seattle to New Orleans to check on Jennifer and my uncle and the rest of my family and on our Amethyst Street house to pack up our belongings. I urgently needed to see for myself the wreckage of the city where I had lived for more than sixty years. Maybe then I could feel close to my beloveds and worry about them.

My son-in-law Chris picked us up at the ghostlike Louis Armstrong Airport. A firefighter, he had stayed in the city on duty, and, until recently, had slept in a huge military barracks with other first responders. Jennifer had recently returned to their home in Algiers from her evacuation spots in New Iberia and later in Houston. I couldn't wait to put my arms around her. After crossing the canal, Chris wrangled the car past fallen wires, downed trees, and flooded cars. No one was directing traffic there, and we entered a no man's land where one flooded house after another lined Pontchartrain Boulevard and the miles of streets near it.

The sun was high in the placid October sky. It was a balmy seventy degrees, and our car windows were down. A half dozen workers maneuvered piles of debris. Trucks, cranes, and grinding machines pulverized trees and branches, relieving the dull landscape with patches of bright yellow sawdust. I smelled wood smoke and nearly choked on some other toxic burning odor. Riding through this strange, desolate land, I was nauseated by thoughts of the havoc this storm had wrought in people's lives here, in my family's lives.

It was hard to believe that a couple of days earlier, I had been strolling the streets of Madrona and Capitol Hill in Seattle, deciding whether to have coffee at Café Verité or a salmon and green onion omelet at the Hi Spot Café as I continued making discoveries in my new city.

The next morning, after spending the night at Chris and Jennifer's with their two excitable brown mini-poodles, Ed and I got an eyeful of the storm's wake in Uptown New Orleans. The assault on the trees on St. Charles Avenue, where I had grown up, seared my heart. The dense oak canopy was now threadbare with so many oak trees down, trees that had been there as long as I could remember. Without the leaves that changed subtly with the seasons from the brilliant mustard-green pollen in the spring to the protective dark-green foliage of winter, there was too much light.

Chris dropped us by our car. He'd parked it on high ground before the storm, around the corner from my parents' house.

We drove across the St. Charles streetcar tracks, dodging heavy branches and oyster shell debris, and passed familiar homes, then turned north on Nashville Avenue toward the Lakefront ten miles away. Within thirty feet, I felt and heard a loud noise coming from the right rear part of the car. Not good. The car was thumping but with a metallic sound. I had to hold the steering wheel firmly to keep us from veering sharply.

I pulled the car over into the debris near the curb. There it was, a tire as flat as a buckwheat pancake. And there we were, in a disaster zone, where normal services like AAA weren't available. I opened the trunk and lifted the lug wrench, but we couldn't find a spare tire. Rattled, I reached for my cell phone and then realized it wouldn't work—and who did I think I would have called?

We decided that I should stay with the car and Ed would walk two miles to the only gas station I could think of at St. Charles and Carrollton. I sat on the curb. An hour passed. An older, white, four-door sedan slowed down near me. The driver parked behind my car and stepped out. He was a lanky, light-skinned African-American man with a spray of freckles across his face and green eyes, maybe thirty years old and about six feet tall.

"I see you have a problem," he said. "Can I help?" He shifted from one foot to another comfortably.

"Yes, I could use some help," I said, opening myself to new circumstances while standing in the middle of old Uptown New Orleans. I took a breath and then another one, conscious that if his skin had been darker I might not have been so open. I pushed aside that thought and thanked him for the opportunity for his help. "My husband is walking to a filling station right now to see about getting the tire fixed."

"Let me look." He lifted the trunk flap and dug around. He emerged and said, "We'll have to take the tire in my car and drive it to Spahr's filling station over on Magazine Street."

"I completely forgot about Spahr's! I used to go there when I lived up this way." It was off the main drag. Had I remembered, poor Ed wouldn't have had to hike the full two miles.

As I looked in dismay at my busted tire, I made the decision to get in the car with this light-skinned, freckled African-American man. I worried about Ed returning and not finding me, so I left a note for him on the windshield. My gut said go, so I climbed into this stranger's front seat and introduced myself.

He introduced himself as well. "My name is Brian. I live with my mother on Perrier Street near Upperline. We've lived there for years."

At the filling station twelve blocks away, I stood by while Brian talked with the mechanic, who showed us the nail Brian had extracted from the tire. He repaired the tire and gave me a couple of repair kits in case it happened again—which was likely since the city streets were strewn with debris, and new potholes were unavoidable. I thanked him and paid with cash. Brian loaded the tire in the trunk and we bounced along Magazine Street, past its boarded-up shops and boutiques. I wistfully noticed two closed coffee shops and fantasized about the decaf soy lattes at C.C.'s.

I said a prayer for the right words and turned to my companion. "Brian, there's no question in my mind, you are an angel and an answer to my prayers for help. Please tell your mother that there are two people out here who are very grateful for your kindness today. I will be looking for a way to pass this kindness forward to someone else."

"Well, yeah, ever since the storm, it's been kinda like being in a special zone." His left hand held the wheel while his right hand worked in rhythm with his speech. "I would want someone to do it for me. And you know," he said, "there have been plenty of good chances for me and everyone else to help others. I think we'll need that for a long time to come."

As we approached St. Charles, I saw Ed standing next to the car. He had returned from his mission having had no luck, and I'm sure he was glad to see me. I introduced him to Brian and filled him in on where we had been. Brian changed the tire, making sure it was firmly in place. He arranged the tools in the trunk and advised us, "Don't forget about the two tire repair kits."

I was tearful when he drove off—this kind young stranger had come to our rescue in a crisis. I knew I would never forget him saying that there would be many more opportunities for the human spirit to shine.

The storm changed the city. It cleared the air. At great cost and sacrifice, it wiped away the illusion that everything would be all right without people paying attention to each other and caring about each other, without realizing that we are all in this together. I began to believe that Katrina's ferocious swipe had cleared the decks for New Orleans to move into the twenty-first century.

During our week in the city, Ed and I packed up the house, one box after another, with some large items set aside for Rebecca, who had lost everything when her ground floor apartment had flooded. October was usually one of my favorite months in New Orleans, but that year, I couldn't get my mind around the overwhelming waste and wreckage beginning just a few blocks away, and the fact that I hadn't been here. I opened one of the patio doors and walked into the garden—the circle of plants around the elderberry tree, the grass that I had spotted from the online satellite photograph we had seen while we sat watching TV news—indicating that the house was standing, as well as the pine tree. On the last day, we stood, drained, in wonder at our good fortune, thinking about Rebecca, temporarily in Austin, Texas, and Jennifer, both dealing with loss, devastation, and frustration along with thousands upon thousands of other New Orleanians. We watched as a moving truck pulled away from the house at the Lakefront, loaded with our belongings—furniture, art, silver and crystal, scrapbooks, kitchenware, Ed's Mongolian hotpot, linens, clothes—headed off for the new life we had started in Seattle. We locked the front door, got in the car, tearfully on my part, waving to the dear Junius children playing across the street, and followed the truck out of the neighborhood. I wondered if Katrina's sweep of the landscape would prompt a cleansing of the city of kings and queens and servants. I found myself hoping so.

Chapter 23

$\mathcal{F}$ORTUNE $\mathcal{T}$ELLER

O ne spring afternoon, after we'd been living in Seattle for a year, the chairperson of Lily's school carnival scheduled for that evening called to ask if I would play the role of fortune teller during the six to eight o'clock time slot. The person who had signed up was sick. Apparently, the chairperson, a friend of Anne Phyfe's, had detected a bit of the "woo-woo" in me when we had talked together at a recent school event, and she thought I would be a good fit. I felt a connection to her bright energy and felt the need for something new and uplifting in my life. My mother had recently died from lung cancer, and I had made regular visits to New Orleans to help with her care. I was ready for some fun. "Yes!" I said enthusiastically. "I'll do it. In fact, it's just what I need! I can't wait!"

After the call, I second-guessed myself for about ten minutes, my mother's voice chasing me. *Oh, you can't do that. That's not you. You'll make a fool of yourself.* Simultaneously, I was already thinking of this gypsy gig with joy, gathering scarves and pieces of clothing and jewelry for my costume. Darn, I could have used that Osiris scepter I hadn't kept after my queenship. Wouldn't that have been a hoot? A little Mardi Gras costuming in Seattle!

An hour before my shift at the fair, I went upstairs to dress for the part. After a few minutes, I knew I was all set, fortified, with favorite objects to wear—a long silver sequined scarf wrapped around a fringed Indian headscarf, ends trailing down my back; dangly earrings; a tortoiseshell whistle; a crescent moon pin with a bright eye and smiling red lips that I'd bought in Jackson, Mississippi, at a music fest where Little Richard played; and two amulets, one worn leather and one beaded garnet that I'd bought in California to honor myself and some of the new ways of being I was growing into.

All this over my big, loose, flax shirt, the brightest shirt I owned, ankle-length skirt, and comfortable sandals. I applied plenty of rouge and lipstick (which felt odd in a city where bare lips are prevalent) and some eyeliner, of which I normally wore precious little. My eyes felt as if they were dancing as I swooped into the living room, where Ed sat reading, and twirled around, bouncing with energy, reminding him I would be home after supper. He swore he was happy staying home rather than wandering in a crowd, and chuckled and admired my garb. I walked out of my house all decked out, scarves around my waist and wrapped around my head, charms and earrings moving with me. I consciously dispelled thoughts that my neighbors might catch me this way. Actually, I was thrilled to be dressing up—an aspect of Mardi Gras that I loved and sorely missed—keenly aware that that dress-up part of me had been neglected for a long time.

I left Ed fixing supper and drove to my granddaughter's school, happy to step into this new arena. Finally, the man who was playing fortune teller before me left his station, and it was my turn to enter the gauzily decorated booth. I sat down, blessed the booth and all who were coming to it, spread out on the tiny table the pink fringed scarf I had brought for this purpose, and arranged my angel cards facedown. Each one-by-two-inch card displayed a printed word and a small image of an angel. My "clients" picked cards with descriptive keywords—brilliance, radiance, starry, heart, love, integrity, truth, joy, delight, or enthusiasm—words to stimulate curiosity, all positive and inspiring, something to talk about if a child picked one up.

Time went out the window. Between six p.m. and 8:23 p.m., I focused on listening to the stream of little people attracted to the mystery of having their fortune told.

A total of sixty kids and one adult visited the booth. I know because they each handed me a carnival ticket that afforded them the opportunity to ask one question. A handful of them had a second or third question and handed me extra tickets. I was in my element and fielded all kinds of queries—a few of which stumped me as to the best way to answer them, though it did seem that most of my customers went away content enough. Popular questions included, Will my friend like me in the future? Will I be a lawyer or a doctor or an artist? Will my mommy's baby be a girl like me? One little girl was upset with her brother and wondered if they would ever get along. Several big sisters interpreted and translated for much younger siblings. One young girl had no question but stated that she missed her grandfather, who had died in March. We held an earnest discussion about missing people and how, after a period of time, she would know that he would always be with her. We talked about the possibility of her being a leader in her family who could ask her mother and brother to meet with her once a week for maybe fifteen minutes to talk about missing him. Two or three children waited in line as our wordy conversation stretched on, and I felt fortunate and humble that we came to a natural closing place before any impatience on my side set in.

In another fortune telling, a boy wanted to know if he would be a famous soccer player, another boy a famous baseball player. When this kind of direct question came up, I found myself saying, "What do you think? Do you have the passion and the discipline to do what it takes to be a champion? I think you have the capability [we'd talk about what that meant]. Won't it be up to you to decide if you want this enough?"

Another boy wanted to know if he would help earth, and I assured him that he would know exactly how to help earth when the time came and that his being conscious about earth today and learning as much as he could every day would be a big help in his quest. Quite a few young ones seemed content to not ask a question but just to sit with me. For them, I generated a few little questions and talked about how they would spread love and light or do great things for the planet, and they would go off with smiles as if reaffirmed.

I believe with almost everyone I managed to say something positive, hopeful, and affirming, and that the young clients felt stronger for the contact.

My granddaughters looked totally puzzled when they saw me in costume, seven-year-old Lily coming back to the booth three times.

"What is my favorite color?" she asked, testing. (Phew, blue; I knew that one.)

"What is my favorite animal?"

"A horse."

"No, Nana, a dolphin!"

Bright, two-year-old Coco sat in the chair, picked up one angel card after another, and handed them to me as if this were her purpose in life. Her father, Bez, stayed nearby, enjoying his break from carrying her around the carnival while Anne Phyfe served up food several booths away. One of Anne Phyfe's friends took a great photograph of Coco sitting in the hot seat with her nana telling her fortune. Anne Phyfe finally had to tell me that the carnival was over, that I could close up.

What a brilliant way to do social work! Tracy and I made a date for the next year—same time, same station. What a gift to look into the eyes of trusting souls and listen. It felt more to me like spreading light than anything I could remember. Bliss! I grinned to myself all the way home to Ed. I could feel the spirit of my sister Penny chuckling at the fun I'd had. I was living *my* life, singing out loud.

Chapter 24

Singing Out Loud

In January of 2006, as I was settling into my new life in Seattle, my sister Pixie called me to come to New Orleans to help with my mother's care. Mom had lung cancer. I was anxious about going. My mother and I had had an awkward relationship for years, but I flew down. During that visit, I washed out Mom's taupe silk camisoles and her pink turbans—the same kind she had worn in the car to Biloxi—helped her change her nightgowns, and fed her sips of water and shaved ice. I also held her feet on this visit and the next one. "Ooooh, that feels so good," she said. "Don't stop."

On the third trip, as I was holding her feet, she let out a yelp of pain. "My back." I climbed onto her bed, my side almost spooning with her, and placed my hands on her back. She whimpered, "Farther down, farther down." I felt her pain in my hands and wrists, and I felt discomfort in my own shoulder from being in a cramped position. And then she was quiet, peaceful, and we lay there together, wordless, touching. I sensed the energy surging through my hands to the affected area. I felt as if we existed in a silky white cocoon. I flew back to Seattle content.

The next month when I entered her room, she said, "Oh good, you're back. Put your hands on my back." My experience of this silent hands-on practice with the mother who loved me but often seemed angry at me was astonishingly healing. No words, just hands. Everything we ever fussed about dissolved with Reiki and touch.

At the end of May, Pixie called. Mom had passed. Surprisingly, I felt blessed, free of complicated emotions. I had grieved for our relationship years before, and I now experienced moments of joy in the midst of fresh grief. *We are healing! We are good! I am grateful—we can continue to heal.*

I climbed the steps to my Seattle office/sanctuary, looking out on the trees in my compact front yard: cypress, witch hazel, magnolia, dogwood, the spindle tree. I sat and began to absorb the fact that Mom was gone, along with yearnings I had had for a warmer relationship with her. It was what it was. I felt grateful for the times I had been in Reiki with her, and I felt amazingly peaceful about her going. I experienced joy that I had received the gift of timelessness with her that seemed to wash away the rough edges between us.

Turning away from the familiar trees that I greeted most days, I looked down at the altar of objects I'd created on the deep windowsill to comfort and inspire me, including a statue of Isis; the bird Thoth, Egyptian god of knowledge (my main writing muse); a carved alder wood vase; an abalone shell holding burned sage; and a photo of Mom dressed up in a Hattie Carnegie cocktail dress and heels about to go out with Crutcher. I loved these touchstones.

In my mind's eye, I saw Mom in the pink turban she had worn in Biloxi and during her last spring days. She wore it like a crown—always a queen. I felt her next to me, the touch of her skin and her silk camisole, her labored breathing, her frailty when I accompanied her into the bathroom. These images flashed repeatedly through my mind, along with the experience of intimacy with her in these moments. We'd had our differences during my life, but she had always shown up and had never physically abandoned me. By moving to California for six months of every year starting thirty years ago, she had set an example for me to leave New Orleans. She appeared much happier on the golf links of Cypress Point with her set of West Coast friends than in New Orleans with its ghosts. I could see her contagious laughter attracting new young friendships in California.

I walked onto our high deck overlooking Lake Washington and turned toward the southern end to behold my sacred Mount Rainier—the awe-inspiring mountain whose small photograph I had displayed on the table next to my bed in New Orleans long before I made the decision to come out here. Now I could see the mountain on any clear day from my bedroom deck. I could leave it again for a while. I would fly to New Orleans for my last trip for Mom.

When I arrived in New Orleans, I drove straight to Betsy's house and organized myself for the couple of days ahead. I walked into Trinity Church where Penny's service had been held three years earlier, where the girls had gone to school next door, where I had plowed ahead with life after my affair with Dale, where I had first facilitated walks on the white-and-purple Chartres-pattern labyrinth. I wasn't quite certain where to sit during the service, then remembered who I was and plunked myself in the front row with Crutcher and my siblings. She had been my mother, too. We sat together in a row listening to traditional hymns she had loved, and when it was over, some of us went down to the crypt where her ashes were placed in a closed cubby next to Penny's.

I would no longer hear what I construed as Mom's criticisms—about Ed, her warning bells about Rebecca's black boyfriend, her disdain for her oldest friend's alcoholism. But I also wouldn't get to hear her loose and playful infectious laughter or see her blue eyes twinkling when she tap danced. I wouldn't ever watch her again in her brilliant blue silk suit, dancing with grandchildren at a grandson's wedding. Or witness her tears flow when she sang along with Jimmy Durante while driving her sky-blue Pontiac convertible. And I wouldn't hear her compassionate comments about other people that she wasn't able to give to herself. And for sure, I would never hear about the pain she must have felt when her brother Garner died as a boy. Or the wretchedness she experienced when breaking up her wartime marriage, and the thousand pinpricks she kept to herself of a mother's suffering over her children's choices and dramas. She was good at concealing her deepest feelings and hadn't shared them with her kids, as far as I knew.

Or at least not with me.

The day after my mother's June 1, 2006 funeral service, I stopped by her house for a farewell look, and the Belgian butler said, "Aren't you coming back to the house for supper?"

I did a double take at the idea—was I invited? The memory of not being invited to the family Christmas dinner at Penny's so long ago flashed across my mind. But I quickly came to. I couldn't imagine not showing up for it.

I returned to the house at six o'clock, arriving before anyone else. I joined sibs and spouses at the large round pedestal table for dinner, even telling a story or two myself, nervous but wanting to take my place there. After dinner, I followed gray-haired and stooped-over Crutcher as my brothers-in-law wheeled him into the library-television room and settled him in his leather reclining chair. Crutcher's sepia oil portrait of his father dominated the room not too far from a much smaller oil self-portrait of his much younger self that I loved.

After my brothers-in-law left the room, I was glad to be alone with Crutcher. I stooped down, looked him in the eye, and told him how grateful I was that he had been a father to me, for the multitude of ways he had provided for me and challenged me to do my best. I said that I knew we'd had awkward times decades ago and again more recently with the suit, but that I also knew he loved me and meant the best for me, and that I loved him despite how difficult it had been for either of us. I told him I was sorry that Mother had left him behind and that he might be lonely without her. Then I squeezed his arm and said, "You have been my greatest teacher. I have learned many life lessons from you." He was such a big force in my life that I'd had to pick myself up over and over, learned to take his perspectives with a grain of salt or have my substance and soul drained out of me. Eventually, I had learned to stand up for myself and go my own way. Without him in my life, I might have disappeared into the woodwork, played the role of deb, queen of the ball, New Orleans wife and mother, and Junior Leaguer forever. So there, in his recliner, I looked at him, with him looking back at me. He looked at me wordlessly through his faded blue eyes. I had no idea whether he comprehended what I was saying; dementia was soon to arise.

The words he had repeatedly preached to me ran through my head: "Stand on your own two feet, Marilee. Stand on your own two feet."

"I'm standing on my own two feet, Crutcher," I said softly. "Thanks to you. Thanks to you." Then I kissed him goodbye on his stubbly cheek and turned to leave.

I walked toward the front door without saying goodbye to the others in the dining room.

At the entrance, as I turned back for a last look around the house where Mom had lived for so many years, a picture of her flashed across my mind again: Mom in the pink turban she had worn during her last spring days. I felt her next to me, the touch of her skin as I lay in bed with her, my hands on her back, the Reiki healing her pain, our distance. And I remembered the last trip to Biloxi she and I had taken.

In late January 2006, the day I arrived for my first visit to her after her diagnosis, she had asked me to drive her to Biloxi to look for the red brick house on the family compound that had been reported missing after Katrina. The next day, she, Rebecca, and I had piled into Mom's silver sedan and took off, Rebecca driving, me next to her. Mom had sat in the back, her posture regal. She looked amazingly elegant in her pink turban and matching coat. Always a queen. We were on a mission to inspect the damage wrought by Katrina to the Biloxi house where she and I had both spent so many summers, summers blessed with being outdoors, playing under the oak, and swimming in the pool, blessed with Nain's consummate way of turning each day into a rhythm of daily rituals—play, eat, swim, crab, nap—and with Nain's loving presence that always steadied me. As memories swirled inside me, she focused what little energy she still possessed on seeing for herself what had happened to the house in Biloxi where she had spent so much of her life as a girl, a young wife, and a mother.

Two and a half hours later, driving down the coastal highway, we passed the relocated block-long casino building we had been told was the marker for the location of the missing house. Rebecca turned off the highway and drove toward the casino. She sat as high as she could in the driver's seat, and her eyes narrowed at the concrete and metal detritus on the ground passing under the car's wheels. How she negotiated Mom's big Lexus through the scattered pieces of rebar and cracked concrete blocks without harm to the car confounded me. She navigated successfully through the debris and turned off the engine. I was glad she was the one driving. I had enough to deal with just trying to comprehend the landscape.

From where I sat, nothing looked familiar, let alone distinguishable—branches, uprooted trees, sheets of corrugated metal, naked wires, wooden shingles, soiled and faded pieces of fabric. The water pushed against what was left of the concrete sea wall, rough enough so that the sound occasionally transmitted across the five-lane highway bed. *Even if the seawall disappears,* I thought, *the water will continue to lap against this shore.* The audible memory of water lapping on the old pier when we went crabbing came to mind. The sky was incongruously blue.

All we had had to go on in our search for the house was the surreal report that an old floating casino a city block long sat on top of it, leaving zero trace of the residential structure. I had watched it on the national news countless times, sometimes in a broadcaster's shocked, insistent voice, and sometimes delivered as if this were ordinary news. Now here it was, not to be believed, the blown-out casino, incongruous, unlatched windows flapping against the exterior, and outrageously out of place. I looked around, subdued. I felt disoriented, nauseated, in disbelief. Floating casinos were supposed to be on barges tethered to pilings—engineered to be safe from storms. Mississippi law stated that these structures could not leave their moorings for cruising. But this casino had succumbed to the massive storm's wind and water and been torn from its barge moorings.

The storm surge had destroyed the barge to which the casino had been tethered. It had swept the structure into the swirling waters whipped up by Hurricane Katrina. The unleashed casino had been transported five hundred yards inland, somehow completely covering the 1847 two-storied, galleried red brick house that had been for a portion of time the property of my grandparents. When Hurricane Camille hit the Gulf Coast in 1969, it had obliterated the handsome white first-floor millwork and the wood flooring, but the big brick structure had stood fast, and in 1975, my grandmother sold the property to the City of Biloxi as a hospitality center. Now—total devastation. No house, no verandah for sipping gin and tonics, no pool for happily splashing children, no garden, no oak for shading wedding parties—nothing in sight but rubble and gray sludge. We three sat in the car silent, appalled, and disoriented, really dumbfounded.

Eventually, Mom said in a low voice, "Go on, you two. I'll stay in the car while you all go look." She slumped against the back seat and said, "I can't do this. Are you sure we're in the right place? It doesn't feel right. I don't recognize a damn thing." She took out a handkerchief and bent her head over her lap. "It's so sad."

Rebecca reached over the seat and wrapped the blue mohair blanket around her grandmother's legs. "Here, Mimi, it's chilly!" she said. "We'll go see what we can find. We'll be back soon. I love you. Call out to us if you need anything at all." Rebecca had been born two years before the house was sold to the City of Biloxi, but she was intensely curious about our connections, our family, and the stories of this place, not the least of which was the wedding of her parents under the big oak.

I turned around to face my mother. "Mom, I'm so sorry—I'm knocked out by this. I can't imagine what it's like for you. The landscape is so changed."

Her eyes closed as if to shut out what she had seen, and she tucked her head down into her chin again. Was she keeping her tears to herself or signaling disapproval? Mom had been married here herself, to my father, twenty-eight summers before Tom and I picked the same spot to wed. She had played here as a child, hunted Indian treasure under the big oak. And she had swum countless laps in the pool that had completely vanished and had swum the mile in the Gulf waters to Deer Island across the way. I waved to her and turned toward the casino, picking my way carefully through the uneven carpet of debris, rattled by the banging of the casino windows, following Rebecca in our search to locate some trace of the house. Still shaken and disoriented, not sure where to head, I had to pay so much attention to where I stepped that I kept losing track of where I was—rubble and broken branches, dirt, and leaves. I looked up at the gigantic rogue casino, previously moored out on the waterfront and now grotesquely out of place, and there it was, the casino, settled on sacred ground, that sound of rows of windows flapping in the cool breeze. It stopped me in my tracks.

After wandering through this no man's land for ten minutes, combing the ground for a clue, I cried out, "Oh my God, Rebecca, over here!" I knelt down on a stretch of a patterned brick path covered mostly by sand. "Look, Rebecca," I said, brushing away the sand, "this is part of the path that led from the dining room in the main house to the brick guest house seventy feet behind it."

"Finally, a clue." She looked toward the wreck. "The bricks of the path disappear underneath the casino."

Archaeologists say that years ago the downstairs of the small guesthouse had been a kitchen staffed with slaves, and the upstairs had provided sleeping quarters for slaves and later servants. Meals once—what, a hundred and fifty years ago, long before my grandparents' ownership—had been prepared in that ten-by-fifteen-foot kitchen, then carried down this path to the main house. I imagined the pots clanging, laughter, and haunting songs.

We spotted two four-foot-high piles of rubble. I recognized one pile of pinkish-red brick on my right as the color of the guesthouse, though the building was nowhere in sight. I flashed on the memory of dancing with Ruth to Papa Celestin's jazz band at my wedding on the patio in front of that house. So many memories—I ached. The other pile of darker red brick I recognized to be the brick of the shingle house near the pool, where our neighbors, the quirky Dr. Esh and his wife, used to live. There had been four houses on our property—the main house, the guesthouse with the downstairs kitchen, the large red-shingle guesthouse, and the caretaker's house—a wooden house on stilts with room underneath for maintenance equipment, where Pocky and Octavia had once lived, and their son, Arthur Bradford, had lived after them. All gone. I discovered more bricks leading to the now-subterranean main house. Rebecca and I each gathered pieces of broken red brick to show Mimi and to bring home as mementos.

As disorienting as all the confusion and disorder was, what really took my breath away was the startling absence of the majestic spreading live oak—the famous three-hundred-year-old oak—and the sound of Biloxi breezes in its branches. The smell of the sea still rolled in, but the smell of the leaves, the moss, and the ferns had vanished. Its hundred-foot canopy of low-slung stout branches had sheltered our play and witnessed so many moments of our lives. I had frequently swum with my sister Pixie directly under the branch that hung over the corner of the swimming pool, pretending to be a mermaid. Years earlier, either Arthur or my uncle had nailed foot-long pieces of wood into its thick trunk. My sibs, cousins, and I used to climb that makeshift ladder into a crevasse, the receiving heart of the tree, where we sat for hours telling stories, our sweat evaporated by the light breezes passing through the branches, a caressing, a rippling, a whisper in my ears, comforting. I had always sworn that I could hear the tree sigh with contentment.

Standing there in the rubble, I invoked the smell of the salt-water mixed with grass and soil and the short, curly moss on the tree. My mind went back to Tom's and my wedding, walking up a freshly mown grass aisle to exchange marriage vows with the man who would become father of my three precious daughters under the biggest, thickest branch where one of our friends, legs wrapped around that branch, took wedding photos. I remembered my mother's often-told story of how she and her sister, Malcolm, had dug for Indian treasure under those sweeping branches. Many years earlier, I had read in a Biloxi newspaper that the tree had provided shade when Indians met for peace talks and council, hence its official live oak registry name, The Councilor Oak. As I stood there, my lungs hurt with the enormous grief from loss of tree and place. This tree had always been a solace to me—permanent, spreading wide and low to the ground.

This huge sheltered casino, maverick and relocated, measuring longer than a city block, had gobbled up everything I held dear here.

"Mom!" Rebecca exclaimed extra loudly over the piles of bricks—so loud because there was little around to absorb the sound of her voice. "How can you bear seeing all this? This was your second home! How in the world are people coping up and down the coast?"

Unfathomable losses racked up trauma and grief in this major earth event. People lost homes, lives, food resources—Katrina's force was so devastating—and surprised the most experienced hurricane rider, wiping away everything in her path. Nothing left. Total eclipse.

I stood there looking at the iron-gray landscape, bleak and forlorn. The casino's dark blue siding caught my eye, along with different shades of brick, red and pink, in piles. This place was my growing ground, my place of tribe, my summer outdoors place, four houses for family—all now reduced to rubble, disintegration, devastation everywhere. As I stood there, with my mother waiting in the car, her handkerchief in hand, facing death and long memories, and my daughter searching for connections to her past, I reeled. I was standing between two worlds.

At first, I felt the dreariness of my environs sapping my energy. Then, my feet firmly planted on the ground, I took in the passing of the old way of life and felt lighter, freer. Even in this eerie quiet, I could see the eclipse would pass—they do—and I sensed that the darkness in this sacred space would give way to light, that after such calamitous desolation and loss, so much death, new life would emerge. The surviving oak trees—in Biloxi, along the Gulf Coast, in New Orleans, and beyond—were bare now, but they would come back, in time. I stood there in the rubble, pondering what the effects of the hurricane meant for me—clearing, change, a nudge to tune my ear to listen, my heart to welcome the new growth that would come.

*E*PILOGUE

I am laughing at myself at the circularity of things. Having thought that when I left New Orleans I would return only to visit, I now live again in the Garden District, doors from the house where I went awry and broke up my young family, a mile down St. Charles Avenue from where I lived with Mother and Crutcher and my five siblings. I now look out the tall windows of my second-floor condo onto the branches of live oak trees—I love the sight and take energy from them. Every now and then, I hear the trumpets and drums of a second line parade inching down the avenue to turn at Washington. I have a front-row seat for the numerous and boisterous Mardi Gras parades with their dancing and marching bands—the ones that start in the Uptown part of the city. Every day I'm amazed at the large groups of tourists from all over the globe who dismount streetcars on my corner to explore the Garden District, Lafayette Cemetery, Commander's Palace, and the large, well-appointed houses of the neighborhood before they hit the small and varied shops on nearby Magazine Street.

In Seattle, I would pick up the glorious *Unfathomable City: A New Orleans Atlas* by Rebecca Solnit and my daughter, Rebecca Snedeker, from my reading table and find myself yearning to connect with the multicultural spiciness of this city, curious to see the changes post-Katrina and to walk along both Audubon Park and City Park paths under fabulous live oaks. I wanted my bones, so joined to New Orleans, to connect again with the flat terrain of live oak trees, magnolias, cypress, crepe myrtles, and candlenut trees.

Highlights of my return include having eight-year-old granddaughter Lulu spend the night with me, and sitting next to her at the New Orleans Museum of Art showing of her mother's documentary film, *By Invitation Only*, and spending the night at the Arnones' to babysit Thomas and Emily, having the nerve to put on a bathing suit to swim in their pool with their friends. I run into people I knew in my former time here and recognize them after thirty or forty years. I'm home.

In the slow unpacking of boxes, I've come across correspondence from my mother, letters and notes in her steady, pretty handwriting, written to me at camp, at school, when I was living away. These reminded me that she was attentive to me in serious ways, always physically present. Thank you, Mom, I loved to read those letters.

Finally, Ed and I have adapted our spousal relationship to new circumstances. He resides in an assisted living facility in New Orleans, while I live here in my spacious condo. We talk every day and see each other often. He misses his sons and some dear friends and breathing in the sweet tang of cedar with the view of Mount Rainier but enjoys the cooking here and is open to new adventures!

My intention in this new chapter of my life is to spend my time delighting myself with my new city and to write about what I find. The thrill of writing at a table near the windows looking out on the oak trees! I own my inability to see things clearly, and writing is one of the ways I move to heal that. And connecting more with my local daughters and their families.

So writing, family, reading, visiting Ed, and exploring this city that is new and remarkable in so many ways—not to say that it's without its challenges—that's what I'm about these days, and I am grateful for the tumultuous journey that has brought me back here.

$\mathcal{A}$CKNOWLEDGMENTS

I've been eager to get to this part of my book. How often I think about the incredible support I have experienced—those who cheered me on, listened to me read stories on a teleconference, reminded me to get up and walk between bouts of writing. Those who wept and laughed with me, who teased me for being so intense, who said when I tried to fit everything that happened to me in these pages, "Save this part for your website. It doesn't fit in the book."

I thank my husband, Ed, and my three brilliant daughters, Anne Phyfe Palmer, Rebecca Snedeker, and Jennifer Arnone.

I thank Tom Snedeker—the father of my daughters, whose love for them is as wide and deep as mine.

I'm grateful to my extended southern family, all those who helped raise me, my girls, and their children, and brought a richness into my existence. Blessed and knowing people: Ruth Nobles, Esther Nobles, Cynthia Nobles Meadoux and family, Pocky and Octavia Bradford, Arthur Bradford, Elmire Bradford, Maude Ellen Bradford, Viola, Theresa, Ruby Wilson, and then Estela Arzu, from Honduras, who brought calm order to my chaotic household at an important time.

Thank you to my favorite teachers: Harriet Ogden, Ruth Sawyer, Mrs. Jarrett, Mrs. Lavigne, and Roberta Capers.

Thank heavens for my Wellesley friends—Jean Kilbourne, Bettie Cartwright, Mary Esther Marshall, and Nancy McDonald Walter—who came back into my life.

Kudos to multiple therapists throughout the years.

Thanks to several men friends—John Petrasch, Peter Van Zandt, and Hans-Henning Erdmann—sweet strong men with integrity, kindness, respect, right thinking. Each one expanded my capacity for relationship.

I honor Norma Freiberg, who mentored me when I cochaired the International Year of the Child Committee and taught me perspective and the value of quiet humor.

Thanks to valued coworkers at Jefferson Parish Human Services Authority in the substance abuse clinic in the 1990s: Randall Rupp, Leslie Tremaine, Chuck Chester, Glen Calvert, Bobette Laurendine, Karen Gerson, Shirley Turco, Rose Ferguson, Marilyn McConnell, Nancy Hirzel, Diana Cormier, Shirley Morlier, and George Morlier.

To the people in my life who have come along and shaken me awake and helped to take off blinders, I am grateful for:

- the baron, for marrying someone else;
- the priest who shook his head when he saw I was incapable of reflecting on the seriousness of the situation I found myself in;
- John Carmody, who both played into old patterns and forced me to face them;
- Suzanne Lacy, who gently and firmly called me "ungrounded" and cautioned me to realize that my work would be useless unless I became grounded;
- the psychic in New Orleans, who urged me to "go now" to Seattle.

I'm grateful to New Orleans friends Elizabeth and Bob Pellegrin, who introduced me to Reiki in the Usui Shiki Ryoho lineage and with whom I still exchange Reiki, and to Chelsea Van Koughnett, Canadian Reiki Master, who gave me my early initiations. And most especially to my Reiki Master, Heidi Gates, who initiated me as a Master, who laughs deeply and loudly and with insight and compassion, whose loving, steady, and brilliant support is still important.

Many thanks to early writing teachers Peter Cooley, Constance Adler, and Nick O'Connell, and to screenwriter Isaac Webb, who inspired me to write down my stories. They provided safe places for sharing my work. And to editor Madeleine Eno, whom I met at my first Northwest Reiki Gathering in Breitenbush Hot Springs, Oregon, whose encouragement, humor, and skill guided me through the first draft of my book.

A few years in, I engaged Kelly Malone, Words Up, as my editor. We worked our way through multiple drafts—fleshing out stories, plumbing emotions, defining scenes, and sharpening dialogue, with Kelly always urging me to go deeper. Many nurturing conversations and laughs later, her friend Mary Lane Potter stepped in. Mary had been teaching me how to write essays, and we had such good time in our sessions, even though she seemed to be asking me to do the impossible. She helped restructure and finesse the book into the form you see now.

I did so much of my writing in our wonderful house with the wide view of Lake Washington in Seattle—I'll always be grateful for the points of view, activism, and genuineness of my neighbors close by: Sarah Banks and Malcolm Harker, Kirk Anderson and Jen Norling, Isabel and Michael Metzger, Jenna Cane and Eric Liu, Ellie David and Mark Sullivan, Barbara Schwartz, Tish Ward, Joan Raskin and Myles Bradley, Martha Brockenbrough and Adam Berliant. Lovable, astute, compassionate people.

I visited several heavenly times with Susie Fitzhugh, a friend/ photographer par excellence, on her property on Vashon Island, walking with her and her dog, Luna, on lush forest paths with wonderful trees. Susie and I grew up together in New Orleans, and it was always so nurturing to have a big Louisiana hug and common language and background of landscape.

I'm grateful for the newer friendship of Mary Turner Henry, beautiful and active Seattle nonagenarian, with whom I found common ground pertaining to our common roots on a certain plantation in St. Joseph, Louisiana.

Other Seattle friends whose support I'm grateful for are Sara Long, Johanna Hedge, Bettiann Wing, Neil MacNeill, Julie Tripp, Mary McGough, Chiara Guerrieri, Melina Meza, Jenny Hayo, Beth Award, Laura Bailey, Irene Ingalls, Danielle Hoffman, Friedemann Schaub, Sharlyn Hidalgo, Viola Brumbaugh, Dean Chier, and Tova Ramer.

I've enjoyed my recent connection with my youngest brother, John Crutcher, and his vivacious and perceptive wife, Encarna, looking out from their home on Puget Sound. I'm grateful that he reached out to me.

And deepest thanks to my beloved Moontime Sisterhood—primary support for a decade: Heidi Gates, Ellen Montague, Madeleine Eno, Arlene Angell, Eileen Sakai, Margaret Anderson, Jessica Paul, Sarah Anderson, Jennifer Wells, Marni Carlson, Lori Gorrell, Ellen Sosinski, Martha Nelson, Rosemary Neff, Dot Patterson, Dawn Hemstreet, DeLynn James, Terry Jordan, Christine Winter, Michele Van Pelt, Karyn Overturf, and Kristin Mihalko.

I had a hard time leaving Viola Brumbaugh's Tai Chi and Xigong classes at her Wild Orchid studio on Capitol Hill in Seattle. I want to give a shout-out to her and to the teachers' classes and workshops I took during the years at my daughter Anne Phyfe's 8 Limbs Yoga Studios. The best!

I rediscovered my New Orleans sisterhood just after Christmas 2017 at a luncheon given by dear friend Mary Sue Nelson

Roniger and attended by Lou Hoffman, Murray Pitts, Susie DeRussy, Erica Labouisse, Elizabeth Jackson, Anne Dean, Ann Loomis, Margaret Nicolson, Patricia Gay, and Nancy Snedeker—familiar friends. I know my happiness at being with them was a factor in deciding to return to New Orleans after thirteen years. Other beloved New Orleans Sisters include Betsy Nalty, Susu Kearney, Jo Harriet Haley (now in Washington, DC), Dian Winingder, Jerry Faulkner (now deceased), Voyce Durling-Jones, Sue Peters, and Stephanie Musser. I have much gratitude for you all.

ABOUT THE AUTHOR

Marilee Eaves grew up in the elite world of Uptown New Orleans, attending Mardi Gras parades and exclusive balls. While away at college, she was twice hospitalized for psychotic episodes. Despite this, she was a magna cum laude graduate of Newcomb College and earned her Master of Social Work from Tulane.

For thirteen years, Marilee lived in the Pacific Northwest, where she developed lifelong women friends and spent time with her oldest daughter's family. Her healing has included writing classes, weaving on a standing loom, and becoming a Reiki Master.

Marilee and her husband live in New Orleans near her younger two daughters and grandchildren. Her articles have been published in New Orleans Museum of Art's *Arts Quarterly*, Episcopal Diocese of Louisiana's *Churchwork*, *Madrona News*, *Touch Magazine*, and *The Awakenings Review*. *Singing Out Loud* is her first book.

www.marileeeaves.com

SELECTED TITLES FROM SHE WRITES PRESS

She Writes Press is an independent publishing
company founded to serve women writers everywhere.
Visit us at www.shewritespress.com.

A Different Kind of Same: A Memoir by Kelley Clink. $16.95, 978-1-63152-999-3. Several years before Kelley Clink's brother hanged himself, she attempted suicide by overdose. In the aftermath of his death, she traces the evolution of both their illnesses, and wonders: If he couldn't make it, what hope is there for her?

All the Ghosts Dance Free: A Memoir by Terry Cameron Baldwin. $16.95, 978-1-63152-822-4. A poetic memoir that explores the legacy of alcoholism and teen suicide in one woman's life—and her efforts to create an authentic existence in the face of that legacy.

Uncovered: How I Left Hassidic Life and Finally Came Home by Leah Lax. $16.95, 978-1-63152-995-5. Drawn in their offers of refuge from her troubled family and promises of eternal love, Leah Lax becomes a Hassidic Jew—but ultimately, as a forty-something woman, comes to reject everything she has lived for three decades in order to be who she truly is.

The Coconut Latitudes: Secrets, Storms, and Survival in the Caribbean by Rita Gardner. $16.95, 978-1-63152-901-6. A haunting, lyrical memoir about a dysfunctional family's experiences in a reality far from the envisioned Eden—and the terrible cost of keeping secrets.

Where Have I Been All My Life? A Journey toward Love and Wholeness by Cheryl Rice. $16.95, 978-1-63152-917-7. Rice's universally relatable story of how her mother's sudden death launched her on a journey into the deepest parts of grief—and, ultimately, toward love and wholeness.

You Can't Buy Love Like That: Growing Up Gay in the Sixties by Carol E. Anderson. $16.95, 978-1631523144. A young lesbian girl grows beyond fear to fearlessness as she comes of age in the '60s amid religious, social, and legal barriers.